Japanese Gamer's Vocab

Gaming and Japanese

Disclaimer and Copyright

Disclaimer of Liability
This book is provided "as is", without warranty of any kind, expressed or implied or otherwise. The author of this book can accept no responsibility for any errors or omissions in this book or any loss, damages, or expense or anything else thereby caused. The use of this book implies you have read this statement.

Fonts
The fonts used in this book are Noto Sans and M PLUS Rounded 1c. These are used under, respectively, the Alpache License, version 2 and the Open Font License.

During the creation of this book, one of the methods the author used to double check various words was the files of the Electronic Dictionary Research and Development Group. The files are under the Creative Commons Attribution-ShareAlike License. Due to the nature of this book being brief definitions, some of the definitions match definitions in the mentioned files as there were cases where a more correct definition in the context of gaming was not possible. Most of the definitions in this books are the author's own and as such do NOT represent the quality of the Electronic Dictionary Research and Development Group's files. This book is NOT endorsed in any way, shape or form by the Electronic Dictionary Research and Development Group whatsoever.

ISBN: 978-1-0879-6869-8

Table of Contents

Table of Contents

Using This Book

This book contains gaming vocab ranging from Rpgs, Fps, and more. The layout of this book is as follows.

In cases where the English definition is brief, the layout goes:

English	Romaji Pronunciation	Japanese

Example:

playthrough	shū me	周目
first playthrough	isshū me	1 周目

When the explanation in English is too long, the layout is as follows:

romaji pronunciation ***Japanese*** **(literal meaning)**

Definition definition definition.

Example:

kansuto カンスト (lit. counter stop)

When a counting variable has reached the maximum and often resets itself, glitches, etc.

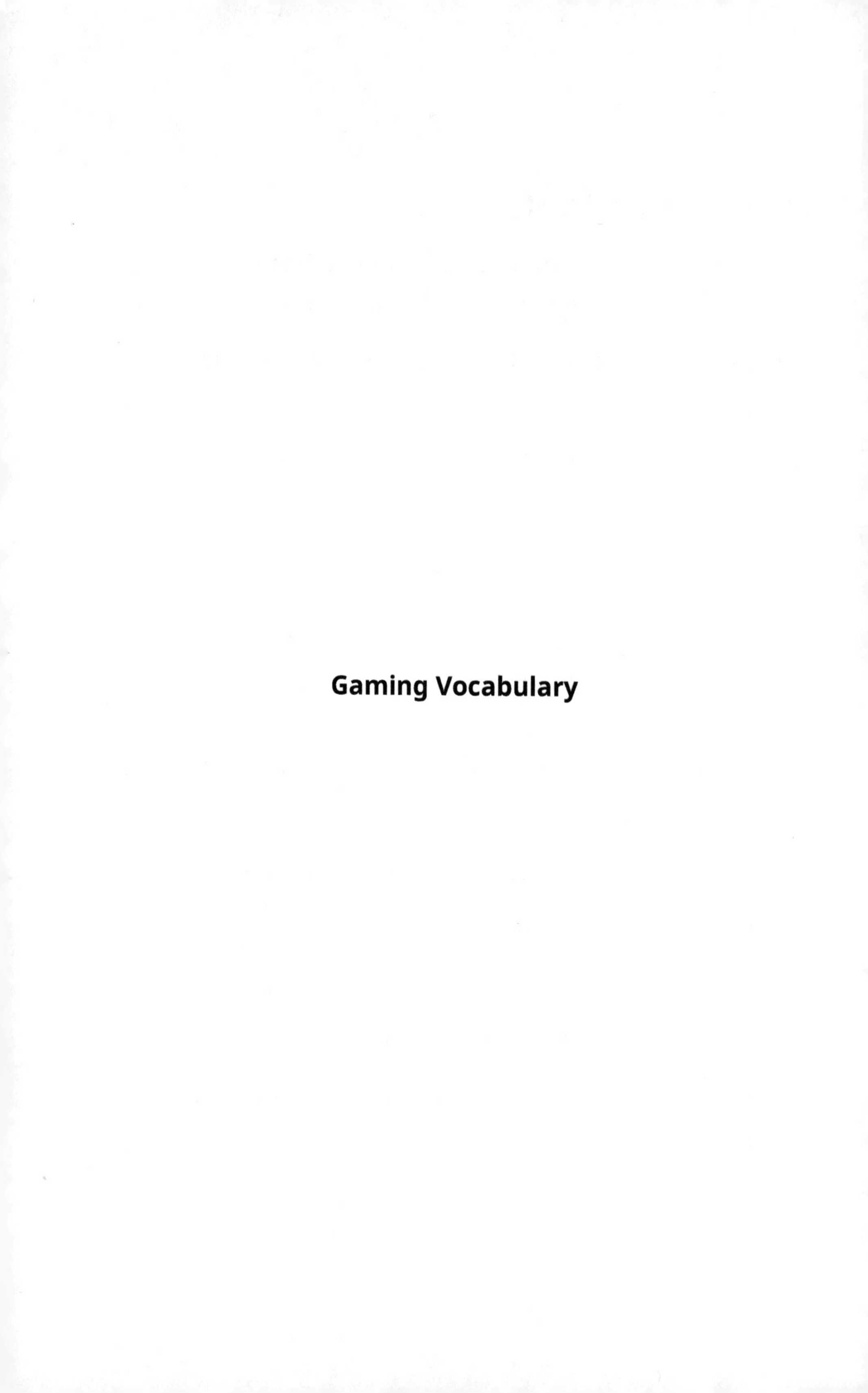

Gaming Vocabulary

1. General Gaming Vocab

Playthroughs and Endings

multiple endings	maruchi endo	マルチエンド
decisions	sentakushi	選択肢
normal ending	nōmaru endo	ノーマルエンド
bad ending	baddo endo	バッドエンド
good ending	guddo endo	グッドエンド
best ending	besuto endo	ベストエンド
replay value	ripurei sei	リプレイ性
high replay value	ripurei sei ga takai	リプレイ性が高い
playthrough	shū me	周目
first playthrough	isshū me	1周目
post-game	kuria go	クリア後
post-game content	kuria go no yōso	クリア後の要素
gameplay	gēmusei	ゲーム性
gameplay	gēmupurei	ゲームプレイ
game design	gēmu dezain	ゲームデザイン
mechanic	mekanikusu	メカニクス
storyline	sujigaki	筋書
main story	mein sutōrī	メインストーリー
linear gameplay	chokusenteki na gēmu purei	直線的なゲームプレイ
level design	reberu dezain	レベルデザイン
good level design	ii reberu dezain	いいレベルデザイン

Saving

save point	sēbu chiten	セーブ地点
save point	sēbu pointo	セーブポイント
(save) password	pasuwādo	パスワード
special password	tokushu na pasuwādo	特殊なパスワード
to save just before boss fight	bosu sen no chokuzen de sēbu suru	ボス戦の直前でセーブする
softlock	tsumi	詰み
to softlock	tsumu	詰む
softlocked save	tsumi sēbu	詰みセーブ
quicksave	chūdan sēbu	中断セーブ
quicksave	kuikku sēbu	クイックセーブ
autosave	ōto sēbu	オートセーブ
save mechanics	sēbu mekanikusu	セーブメカニクス
save system	sēbu shisutemu	セーブシステム

Combat

battle	sentō	戦闘
battle field	sentō gamen	戦闘画面
to fight	tatakau	戦う
be defeated	taoreru	倒れる
to beat	taosu	倒す
move / attack	waza	技

attack	kōgeki	攻撃
to attack	kōgeki suru	攻撃する
opponent	aite	相手

Damage

damage	damēji	ダメージ
to deal damage	damēji o ataeru	ダメージを与える
to damage an opponent	aite ni damēji o ataeru	相手にダメージを与える
to take damage	damēji o ukeru	ダメージを受ける
to not take damage	damēji o ukenai	ダメージを受けない
non-damaging	damēji o ataenai	ダメージを与えない

Health

health	tairyoku	体力
enemy with a lot of health	tairyoku no ōi teki	体力の多い敵
remaining health	nokori tairyoku	残り体力
healthbar	raifu gēji	ライフゲージ
meter (e.g. stamina)	gēji	ゲージ
healthpoint	herusu pointo	ヘルスポイント
healing location	kaifuku basho	回復場所

Enemies

enemy	teki	敵
weak enemies	zako	雑魚
strongest	saikyō	最強
invincible	muteki	無敵
to defeat an enemy	teki o taosu	敵を倒す
difficult to defeat enemy	taoshinikui teki	倒しにくい敵
to underestimate	nameru	なめる
to touch an enemy	teki ni butsukaru	敵にぶつかる
a nearby enemy	chikaku ni iru teki	近くにいる敵
enemy movement pattern	teki no idō patān	敵の移動パターン
enemy attack pattern	teki no kōgeki patān	敵の攻撃パターン
to be surrounded by enemies	teki ni kakomareta	敵に囲まれた
group (of enemies)	shūdan	集団

Boss

boss	bosu	ボス
to beat	taosu	倒す
boss battle	bosu sen	ボス戦
before the boss	bosu mae	ボス前
miniboss	mini bosu	ミニボス

event boss	ibento bosu	イベントボス
final boss	rasubosu	ラスボス
form	sugata	姿
I beat the final boss!	rasubosu o taoshita!	ラスボスを倒した！
hidden boss	kakushi bosu	隠しボス
true final boss	shin rasubosu	真ラスボス
unbeatable boss fight	taosenai bosu	倒せないボス

Movement and Actions

to move	idō suru	移動する
to control	sōsa suru	操作する
jump	jampu	ジャンプ
to jump	jampu suru	ジャンプする
double jump	nidan jampu	二段ジャンプ
jump bug	jampu bagu	ジャンプバグ
to crouch	shagamu	しゃがむ
to examine	shiraberu	調べる
to perform	okonau	行う
to explore	tanken suru	探検する
to glide	kakkū suru	滑空する
to warp	wāpu suru	ワープする

Stage

stage (level)	sutēji	ステージ
the final stage	saishū sutēji	最終ステージ
to beat (game / stage)	kuria suru	クリアする
clear rate	kuria ritsu	クリア率
to beat a game	gēmu o kuria suru	ゲームをクリアする
countword for stages	men	面

Environment and Field

environment	kankyō	環境
to destroy the environment	kankyō hakai o suru	環境破壊をする
environmental damage	kankyō damēji	環境ダメージ
the field	fīrudo	フィールド
procedural generation	jidō seisei	自動生成
point on the map	chiten	地点
boundary	kyōkai	境界
teleporter	terepōtā	テレポーター
teleport	terepōto	テレポート
fast travel	fasuto toraberu	ファストトラベル
destination	mokutekichi	目的地
map	mappu	マップ

point (on the map)	chiten	地点
minimap	minimappu	ミニマップ
red dot	akaten	赤点
displayed on the minimap	minimappu ni hyōji sarete iru	ミニマップに表示されている
2D	tsū dī	2D
2-dimensional	nijigen	二次元
flat (2D)	heimen	平面
2.5D	ni ten go jigen	2.5 次元
3D	surī dī	3D
3D	sanjigen	三次元
3D model	sanjigen moderu	三次元モデル

Camera

the camera	kamera	カメラ
to move the camera	kamera o idō suru	カメラ移動する
to control the camera	kamera o sōsa suru	カメラを操作する
to turn	hanten suru	反転する
camera angle	kamera anguru	カメラアングル
camera height	kamera no takasa	カメラの高さ
camera distance	kamera no kyori	カメラの距離
camera position	kamera ichi	カメラ位置
camera orientation	kamera muki	カメラ向き
camera movement	kamera idō	カメラ移動
first person view	ichininshō shiten	一人称視点
third person view	sanninshō shiten	三人称視点
camera that doesn't move	idō dekinai kamera	移動できないカメラ

fixed camera	kotei shite iru kamera	固定しているカメラ
camera speed	kamera sokudo	カメラ速度
zoom	zūmu	ズーム
zoom-out	zūmu auto	ズームアウト
side scrolling camera	yoko sukorōru no kamera	横スクロールのカメラ

Bugs and Glitches

Easter egg	īsutā eggu	イースターエッグ
Easter egg	kakushi kinō	隠し機能
hidden message	kakushi messēji	隠しメッセージ
bug / glitch	bagu	バグ
buggy / glitchy	bagui	バグい
full of bugs	bagu ga ōi	バグが多い
to glitch	baguru	バグる
to freeze	furīzu suru	フリーズする
glitch	guricchi	グリッチ
cheat	chīto	チート
cheat code	chīto komando	チートコマンド
hidden cheat	kakushi komando	隠しコマンド
exploit	urawaza	裏技
bug exploit	bagu waza	バグ技

eipa 永パ (lit. eternal pattern)

A special type of exploit used to usually gain an advantage such as excessive amount of lives or to stall, etc. It was especially useful in the arcade era where someone could effectively hog the machine by never getting a game over.

kansuto カンスト (lit. counter stop)

When a counting variable has reached the maximum and often resets itself, glitches, etc.

mugen zōshoku 無限増殖 (lit. infinite increase)

Exploit to get an infinite number of an item or lives

anzenchitai 安全地帯 (lit. safe area)

(Often times) glitched area where you won't take damage, often used in boss fights

item clone (glitch)	aitemu chōfuku	アイテム重複
debug	debaggu	デバッグ
debug mode	debaggu mōdo	デバッグモード
code to enter debug mode	debaggu komando	デバッグコマンド

Speedrunning and Challenges

yarikomi やり込み
challenge / special runthrough (e.g. no level ups)

owata shiki オワタ式
challenge where if you get hit once, you fail

...kinshi...禁止
no... (healing, etc.)

speedrun	supīdo ran	スピードラン
sequence breaking	shīkensu bureiku	シーケンスブレイク
real-time attack	riaru taimu atakku	リアルタイムアタック
loading time	rōdo jikan	ロード時間

Unlockable

unlockable	anrokku kanō	アンロック可能
to unlock a character	kyara o anrokku suru	キャラをアンロックする
to unlock (e.g. skill)	anrokku suru	アンロックする
hidden character	kakushi kyara	隠しキャラ
unlockable (lit. bonus) character	bōnasu kyara	ボーナスキャラ

Types of Gamers

Hardcore and Casual

hardcore gamer	hādokoa gēmā	ハードコアゲーマー

koa gēmā コアゲーマー (lit. core gamer)

Extremely interested in games, the type of person to say you are not a true gamer if you play such and such popular / casual game.

hebī gēmā ヘビーゲーマー (lit. heavy gamer)

Tend to focus really hard on one game and get all the collectibles, speedruns, etc. and are incredible at the game but don't play a huge variety of games. Always play multiple playthroughs.

to 100% a game	hyaku pāsento kuria suru	100パーセントクリアする
second playthrough	ni shū me	2周目
casual gamer	kajuaru gēmā	カジュアルゲーマー

midoru gēmā ミドルゲーマー(lit. middle gamer)

In between light gamer and heavy gamer, most people are probably this. Tend to game as a hobby.

raito gēmā ライトゲーマー(lit. light gamer)

Play a variety of games and tend not to 100% games or do second playthroughs. Play games for enjoyment and play on normal mode rather than hardmode. Tends to enjoy things related to games such as magazines. Tend to watch gaming reviews before buying one.

nuru gēmā ヌルゲーマー

Prefers easy games.

Other

tsumi gēmā 積みゲーマー
Prefer to have a lot of games.
āru pī gēmā RP ゲーマー
RPG gamer
sutōrī jūshiha ストーリー重視派
Someone who plays games for the story
ākēdo gēmā アーケードゲーマー
arcade gamer
kaku gēmā 格ゲーマー
fighting game gamer
oto gēmā 音ゲーマー
rhythm game gamer
pasokon gēmā パソコンゲーマー
PC gamer
konsōru gēmā コンソールゲーマー
console gamer
kusogē hantā クソゲーハンター
Try to find the crappiest games to play and laugh at how stupid and glitchy the games are.

Misc

video game	gēmu	ゲーム
gamer	gēmā	ゲーマー
retrogame	retorogēmu	レトロゲーム
retrogame	regē	レゲー
nostalgic	natsukashii	懐かしい
player	pureiyā	プレイヤー
your character	jiki	自機
life	ki	機
number of lives	ki sū	機数
cutscene	mūbi	ムービー
(full word) cutscene	mūbīshīn	ムービーシーン
long cutscene	nagai mūbī	長いムービー
during the cutscene	mūbī chū	ムービー中
ending (cutscene)	endingu	エンディング
loading screen	rōdo gamen	ロード画面
pause	pōzu	ポーズ
pause screen	pōzu game	ポーズ画面
to resume	saikai suru	再開する
to skip	sukippu suru	スキップする
quick time event	kuikku taimu ibento	クイックタイムイベント
puzzle	nazo	謎
puzzle solution	nazotoki	謎解き
to solve a puzzle	nazo o toku	謎を解く
hint	hinto	ヒント
guide/walkthrough	kōryaku	攻略

strategy guide book	kōryakubon	攻略本
game mode	gēmu mōdo	ゲームモード
adventure	adobenchā	アドベンチャー
versus	bāsasu	VS
gamer's thumb	gēmā oyayubi	ゲーマー親指
beginning of the game	joban	序盤
resetting until you get what you want	risetto marason	リセットマラソン
resetting until you get what you want	rise mara	リセマラ
tutorial	chūtoriaru	チュートリアル
end of the game	shūban	終盤
gameover	gēmuōbā	ゲームオーバー
gameover screen	gēmuōbā gamen	ゲームオーバー画面
respawn	risupōn	リスポーン
minigame	minigēmu	ミニゲーム
to beat (minigame)	shōri suru	勝利する
soundtrack	saundo torakku	サウンドトラック
character creation	kyara meiku	キャラメイク
character creation screen	kyara meiku gamen	キャラメイク画面

2. Items

General

item	aitemu	アイテム
item's ability	aitemu no seinō	アイテムの性能
effect	kōka	効果
place where you obtain an item	nyūshu basho	入手場所
to respawn (item / weapon)	saishutsugen suru	再出現する
respawn time (item / weapon)	saishutsugen jikan	再出現時間

Common Items

map	mappu	マップ
to view map	mappu o miru	マップを見る
recovery	kaifuku	回復
healing item	kaifuku aitemu	回復アイテム
full recovery	zenkaifuku	全回復
potion	pōshon	ポーション
revival item	fukkatsu aitemu	復活アイテム
currency	tsūka	通貨
gold (currency)	gōrudo	ゴールド
to not have enough gold	gōrudo ga tarinai	ゴールドが足りない
treasure chest	takarabako	宝箱

to open a treasure chest	takarabako o akeru	宝箱を開ける
inside the treasure chest	takarabako no nakami	宝箱の中身

Types

power-up	pawā appu	パワーアップ
consumable item	shōmō aitemu	消耗アイテム
hidden item	kakushi aitemu	隠しアイテム
collectible	shūshū aitemu	収集アイテム
equipment	sōbi	装備
accessory	akusesarī	アクセサリー

Inventory

inventory	imbentori	インベントリ
inventory system	imbentori shisutemu	インベントリシステム
limited inventory	seigen imbentori	制限インベントリ
unlimited inventory	mugen imbentori	無限インベントリ
starting gear	shoki sōbi	初期装備
to select	sentaku suru	選択する
to equip	sōbi suru	装備する
inventory management	inbentori kanri	インベントリ管理
inventory sorting	inbentori seiri	インベントリ整理
item clone (glitch)	aitemu chōfuku	アイテム重複

Actions

to hold	motsu	持つ
to let go of	tebanasu	手放す
to throw	nageru	投げる
to use an item	aitemu o shiyō suru	アイテムを使用する
to put away (an item)	hokan shite oku	保管しておく
to equip	sōbi suru	装備する
to pick up an item	aitemu o hirou	アイテムを拾う
to obtain an item	aitemu o shutoku suru	アイテムを取得する
to get an item	te ni ireru	手に入れる
to collect an item	aitemu o kaishū suru	アイテムを回収する
to collect items	shūshū suru	収集する
to drop an item	aitemu o doroppu suru	アイテムをドロップする
to drop an item (enemy drop)	aitemu o otosu	アイテムを落とす
to discard	suteru	捨てる

3. Menu

General

menu	menyū	メニュー
to close (the menu)	tojiru	閉じる
to move between menus	utsuru	移る
to select	sentaku suru	選択する
to confirm	kakunin suru	確認する
confirm / OK	kettei	決定
cancel	kyanseru	キャンセル
return	modoru	戻る

Saving

to save	sēbu suru	セーブする
saving...	sēbuchū	セーブ中
slot	surotto	スロット
file	fairu	ファイル
to save (a file)	hozon suru	保存する
save data	sēbu dēta	セーブデータ
to overwrite	uwagaki suru	上書きする
to initialize	shokika suru	初期化する
Is it really okay?	hontō ni yoroshii desu ka?	本当によろしいですか？
to delete	shōjo suru	消除する
to transfer	ikō suru	移行する

autosave	ōto sēbu	オートセーブ
autosave function	ōto sēbu kinō	オートセーブ機能

Load

load	rōdo	ロード
to load	rōdo suru	ロードする
save data	sēbu dēta	セーブデータ
loading...	rōdo chū	ロード中
to finish	kanryo suru	完了する

Home

restart (console)	saikidō	再起動
update	appudēto	アップデート
to update	kōshin suru	更新する
to erase (eg data)	shōkyo suru	消去する

Main Menu

main menu	mein menyū	メインメニュー
to open the main menu	mein menyū o hiraku	メインメニューを開く
title menu	taitoru menyū	タイトルメニュー
title screen	taitoru gamen	タイトル画面
to return to title menu	taitoru menyū ni modoru	タイトルメニューに戻る

new game	hajimekara	はじめから
begin	hajimeru	はじめる
continue	tsuzukikara	つづきから
play	purei	プレイ
start	sutāto	スタート
mode	mōdo	モード
adventure	adobenchā	アドベンチャー
versus	bāsasu	VS
chapter select	chaputā sentaku	チャプター選択
chapter	shō	章
new chapter	shinshō	新章
gallery	gyararī	ギャラリー
cutscene	mūbī	ムービー
soundtest	saundo tesuto	サウンドテスト

Pause Menu

pause	pōzu	ポーズ
pause menu	pōzu menyū	ポーズメニュー
pause screen	pōzu gamen	ポーズ画面
to display the pause menu	pōzu menyū o hyōji suru	ポーズメニューを表示する
to open the pause menu	pōzu menyū o hiraku	ポーズメニューを開く
settings	settei	設定
option	opushon	オプション
save	sēbu	セーブ
load	rōdo	ロード

end / quit	shūryō	終了

Game Over

game over	gēmu ōbā	ゲームオーバー
a continue	kontinyū	コンティニュー
return to title screen	taitoru ni modoru	タイトルに戻る
continue	tsuzuki	続き

Settings

settings	settei	設定
option	opushon	オプション
to select	sentaku suru	選択する
to change	henkō suru	変更する
audio	ōdio	オーディオ
stereo	sutereo	ステレオ
mono	mono / monoraru	モノ／モノラル
sound effect	kōkaon	効果音
music	ongaku	音楽
voice	serifu	セリフ
subtitles	jimaku	字幕
Japanese subtitles	nihongo jimaku	日本語字幕
English subtitles	eigo jimaku	英語字幕
controls	sōsa	操作
control settings	sōsa settei	操作設定

control scheme	sōsa hōhō	操作方法
sensitivity	kando	感度
difficulty	nan'ido	難易度
difficulty settings	nan'ido settei	難易度設定
easy	kantan	簡単
normal	futsū	普通
normal	nōmaru	ノーマル
hard	muzui	むずい
hard mode	hādo mōdo	ハードモード
high difficulty	kō nan'ido	高難易度

4. Online and Multiplayer

General Online

account	akaunto	アカウント
new account	shin akaunto	新アカウント
multiple accounts	fukusū no akaunto	複数のアカウント
to use multiple accounts	fukusū no akaunto o riyō suru	複数のアカウントを利用する
suspended	teishi	停止
account suspension	akaunto tōketsu	アカウント凍結
log in	rogu in	ログイン
log in screen	rogu in gamen	ログイン画面
log out	roguauto	ログアウト
password	pasuwādo	パスワード
enter password	pasuwādo nyūryoku	パスワード入力
change password	pasuwādo henkō	パスワード変更
please enter your password	pasuwādo o nyūryoku shite kudasai	パスワードを入力してください
user	yūzā	ユーザー
username	yūzā na	ユーザー名
cross-save	kurosusēbu	クロスセーブ
crossplay	kurosu purei	クロスプレイ
online game (net game)	netto gēmu	ネットゲーム
online game	netoge	ネトゲ

online game	onrain gēmu	オンラインゲーム
server	sābā	サーバー
to select a server	sābā o sentaku suru	サーバーを選択する
server (joke writing)	saba	鯖
server	saba	サバ
offline	ofurain	オフライン
to go AFK	riseki suru	離籍する
AFK	riseki chū	離籍中
idle	hōchi	放置
to disconnect	setsudan suru	切断する
to drop connection	ochiru	落ちる
to fall asleep and lose connection	neochi	寝落ち
lag	ragu	ラグ
to lag	raguru	ラグる
laggy	ragui	ラグい
full of lag	ragu ga ōi	ラグが多い
error	erā	エラー
server crash	sābā kurasshu	サーバークラッシュ
congestion	konzatsu	混雑
LAN	ran	ＬＡＮ
LAN adapter	ran adaputā	LAN アダプター
LAN cable	ran kēburu	LAN ケーブル
modem	modemu	モデム
router	rūtā	ルーター
ping	pingu chi	PING 値
patch	pacchi	パッチ
day 1 patch	dei wan pacchi	デイワンパッチ

Multiplayer

singleplayer	shinguru	シングル
singleplayer	soro purei	ソロプレイ
one player	hitori pureī	１人プレイ
multiplayer	maruchipureiya	マルチプレイヤ
multiplayer	maruchipurē	マルチプレー
multiplayer	maruchi	マルチ
number of players	purei sū	プレイ数
maximum number of players	saidai ninzū	最大人数
offline multiplayer	ofurain maruchi	オフラインマルチ
bot	botto	ボット
splitscreen	gamen bunkatsu	画面分割
LAN party	ran pātī	LAN パーティー
co-op	kyōryoku purei	協力プレイ
team based (game)	chīmu purē	チームプレー
friendly fire	dōshi uchi	同士討ち
team kill	chīmu kiru	チームキル
to contribute to your team	chīmu ni kōken suru	チームに貢献する
assist	ashisuto	アシスト
during the match	taisenchū	対戦中
opponent	aite	相手
to damage an opponent	aite ni damēji o ataeru	相手にダメージを与える

Cheating

to report	tsūhō suru	通報する
cheat	chīto	チート
cheater	chītā	チーター
countermeasure (against cheats)	taisaku	対策
permaban	eikyū ban	永久 BAN
macro	makuro	マクロ

Chat and Friends

chat	chatto	チャット
voice chat	boisu chatto	ボイスチャット
to mute someone	myūto ni suru	ミュートにする
to ignore	mushi suru	無視する
message	messēji	メッセージ
to send a message	messēji o sōshin suru	メッセージを送信する
to register a friend	furendo tōroku suru	フレンド登録する
friend request	furendo boshū	フレンド募集
party	pātī	パーティー
to send a game invitation	shōtai o sōshin suru	招待を送信する
to join	sanka suru	参加する

to invite (an online player)	boshū suru	募集する

Matchmaking

matchmaking with strangers	nora	野良
ranked match	ranku macchi	ランクマッチ
match	shiai	試合
lobby	robī	ロビー
online matchmaking	netto taisen	ネット対戦
PvP	taijinsen	対人戦
room (online)	rūmu	ルーム
to create a room	rūmu o sakusei suru	ルームを作成する
to enter a room	nyūshitsu suru	入室する
time remaining (in the match)	nokori jikan	残り時間

Trolling

to grief / troll	aoru	煽る
griefing / trolling	aori	煽り
to rage	abareru	暴れる
sore loser	makeoshimi	負け惜しみ
salty (angry)	buchigire	ブチギレ

Chat slang

asdfghjkl (random typing)	fujiko	くぁｗせｄｒｆｔｇｙふじこｌｐ
n00b	zako	雑魚
gg	otsu	乙
gg n00b!	zako otsu	雑魚乙
lol gg n00b!	zako otsu	雑魚乙 ww
owning noobs	zakokari	雑魚狩り
trash	gomi	ゴミ
salty (extremely angry)	buchigire	ブチギレ
lol	warai	笑
ragequitter	setsudanchū	切断厨

5. Stream

stream	haishin	配信
streamer	haishinsha	配信者
live streaming	raibu haishin	ライブ配信
livestream	nama haishin	生配信
to stream	haishin suru	配信する
to send out (a stream)	hasshin suru	発信する
Let's Play	jikkyō purei	実況プレイ
stream sniping	sutorīmu sunaipu	ストリームスナイプ
comment	komento	コメント
comment	kome	コメ
"first comment!"	ichi kome	いちこめ
subscriber	tōrokusha	登録者
subscription	tōroku	登録
to subscribe	tōroku suru	登録する
clickbait	kurikku beito	クリックベイト
clickbait title	taitoru sagi	タイトル詐欺
thumbnail	samune	サムネ
clickbait thumbnail	samune sagi	サムネ詐欺
capture card	kyapuchā bōdo	キャプチャーボード
AV adapter	ei bui adaputā	AV アダプター
compilation / montage	shū	集
compilation of all the boss battles (video)	zen bosu senshū	全ボス戦集

highlights	kōpureishū	好プレイ集
combo montage	kombo shū	コンボ集
clip	kurippu	クリップ
clip	tanpen	短編
clip compiliation	tanpen shū	短編集
(unedited)	muhenshū	【無編集】
first time playing game	shoken purei	初見プレイ
first time playing game	shokai purei	初回プレイ
spoiler	netabare	ネタバレ
I hate spoilers	netabare kirai	ネタバレ嫌い
contains spoilers!	netabare ari	ネタバレあり
spoiler warning	netabare chūi	ネタバレ注意
thumbnail spoiler	samunebare	サムネバレ
no spoilers!	netabare kinshi	ネタバレ禁止！

6. Describing

General

graphics	gurafikku	グラフィック
development	tenkai	展開
to be influenced by	ni eikyō o ukeru	に影響を受ける
character design	kyarakutā dezain	キャラクターデザイン
character design	kyaradeza	キャラデザ
game design	gēmu dezain	ゲームデザイン
game designer	gēmu dezainā	ゲームデザイナー
game balance	gēmu baransu	ゲームバランス
system seller / killer game	kirā taitoru	キラータイトル
release date	hatsubaibi	発売日
publisher	mēkā	メーカー
genre	janru	ジャンル
platform	purattohōmu	プラットホーム
region free	rījon furī	リージョンフリー
region code	rījon kōdo	リージョンコード

Releasing

title (of game)	taitoru	タイトル
series	shirīzu	シリーズ
first game in the series	daiissaku	第一作
sequel	zokuhen	続編

the original game (the first game in the series)	shodai	初代
...th installation	sakume	作目
the second installation	ni sakume	２作目
sequel	zokuhen	続編
direct sequel	kanzen zokuhen	完全続編
trailer	torērā	トレーラー
story trailer	sutōrī torērā	ストリートレーラー
gameplay trailer	gēmu purei torērā	ゲームプレイトレーラー

Version

new release	shinsaku	新作
pre-purchase	yoyaku kōnyū	予約購入
English version	eigoban	英語版
overseas edition	kaigaiban	海外版
dubbing	dabingu	ダビング
North American Version	Hokubeiban	北米版
Japanese version	Nihonban	日本版
beta-version	bēta ban	ベータ版
beta-test participants	bēta tesuto sankasha	ベータテスト参加者
beta-tester	bēta tesutā	ベータテスター
closed beta	kurōzudo bēta	クローズドベータ
test version	tesuto ban	テスト版

early access	sōki akusesu	早期アクセス
paid trial version	yūryō taikenban	有料体験版
released version	rirīsu ban	リリース版
release version	seihinban	製品版
demo / trial version	taikenban	体験版
pc version	pī shī ban	PC 版
computer version	pasokonhan	パソコン版
(console) version	(gēmuki)han	（ゲーム機）版

Gameplay

gameplay	gēmusei	ゲーム性
gameplay	gēmu purei	ゲームプレイ
experience	taiken	体験
boring experience	taikutsu na taiken	退屈な体験
immersion	botsunyūkan	没入感
atmospheric game	fun'iki gē	雰囲気ゲー
visuals	bijuaru	ビジュアル
realistic	rinjōkan no aru	臨場感のある
realistic graphics	riaru na gurafikku	リアルなグラフィック
cinematic	eigappoi	映画っぽい
story	sutōrī	ストーリー
poor story	yowai sutōrī	弱いストーリー
game engine	gēmu enjin	ゲームエンジン
physics engine	butsuri enjin	物理エンジン
physics	butsuri	物理
mechanics	mekanikusu	メカニクス
system	shisutemu	システム

combat system	sentō shisutemu	戦闘システム
growth system	seichō shisutemu	成長システム
movement system	idō shisutemu	移動システム
save system	sēbu shisutemu	セーブシステム

7. Genres

General

genre	janru	ジャンル
action	akushon	アクション
stealth	suterusu	ステルス
shooter	shūtingu gata	シューティングゲーム
FPS	fāsuto pāson shūting gēmu	ファーストパーソンシューティング
third person shooter	sādo pāson shūtingu	サードパーソンシューティング
adventure	adobenchā	アドベンチャー
platformer	purattofōmu gēmu	プラットフォームゲーム
horror game	horā gēmu	ホラーゲーム
survival horror	sabaibaru horā	サバイバルホラー
puzzle	pazuru	パズル
falling block puzzle game	ochimono pazuru	落ち物パズル
falling block game	ochi gē	落ちゲー
online game	netoge	ネトゲ
mobile game	mobairugēmu	モバイルゲーム
free to play	kihon muryō	基本無料
simulation	esu eru jī	SLG
sports	supōtsu	スポーツ
racing	rēsu	レース

dating sim	ren'ai gēmu	恋愛ゲーム
dating sim	otome gēmu	乙女ゲーム
dating sim	otome gē	乙女ゲー
sandbox game	hakoniwa gēmu	箱庭ゲーム
retro	retoro	レトロ
retrogame	retorogēmu	レトロゲーム
retrogame	regē	レゲー
indie game	indī gēmu	インディーゲーム

Rpg Types

RPG	āru pī jī	RPG
RPG	rō pure	ロープレ
MMO	taninzū dōji sankagata onrain gēmu	多人数同時参加型オンラインゲーム
MMORPG	daikibo taninzū dōji sanka gata onrain āru pī jī	大規模多人数同時参加型オンライン RPG
MOBA	moba	MOBA
Hack and Slash	hakku ando surasshu	ハックアンドスラッシュ
Hack and Slash	hakusura	ハクスラ
Rogue-Like	rōgu raiku	ローグライク
strategy game (lit. strategy simulator)	senryaku shimyurēshon	戦略シミュレーション
strategy game	senryaku esu eru jī	戦略 SLG
real time strategy	riarutaimusutoratejī	リアルタイムストラテジー

Turn Base Strategy	tānseisutoratejī	ターン制ストラテジー
tower defense	tawā difensu	タワーディフェンス
defense game	bōei gēmu	防衛ゲーム

Arcade Game Types

arcade game	ākēdo gēmu	アーケードゲーム
side scrolling beat'em up	berutosukurōru	ベルトスクロール
beat'em up	berusuku	ベルスク
shooter	shūtingu gata	シューティングゲーム
sidescrolling shooter	yoko sukurōru shūtingu	横スクロールシューティング
verticle scrolling shooter	tate sukurōru shūtingu	縦スクロールシューティング
rail shooter game	gan shūtingu gēmu	ガンシューティングゲーム
music / rhythm game	otogē	音ゲー
rhythm game	rizumu gē	リズムゲー
dot eater game	dotto īto	ドットイート
racing game	rēsu gēmu	レースゲーム
fighting game	kakugē	格ゲー

Esports Genres

esports	ī supōtsu	e スポーツ
First-Person Shooter	fāsuto pāson shūtingu gēmu	ファーストパーソンシューティングゲーム
MOBA	moba	MOBA
Fighting game	kaku gē	格ゲー

Other

open world	ōpunwārudo	オープンワルド
freemium	furīmiamu	フリーミアム
singleplayer	soro purei	ソロプレイ
multiplayer	maruchipurei	マルチプレイ
Co-op	kyōryoku purei	協力プレイ
joke game	bakagē	バカゲー
crappy game	kusogē	クソゲー
to glitch	baguru	バグる

murigē 無理ゲー

extremely difficult / impossible-to-beat game

shini gē 死にゲー

game where it is easy to die in

oboegē 覚えゲー

game that requires memorization to beat a level, etc

shokengoroshi 初見殺し

when the creators troll the player by creating a deceptively easy to die element in the game, such as a high level enemy early game or something that shouldn't kill you but does

nurugē ヌルゲー

easy-to-beat game

pochi gē ポチゲー

game where you cannot die / non-stressful game / casual game

yūjō hakai gēmu 友情破壊ゲーム

game that will ruin your friendship

utsu gē 鬱ゲー

depressing / dark game

well made game	ryō gē	良ゲー
poorly ported / remade / localized game	rekka gē	劣化ゲー
localization	rōkaraizu	ローカライズ

8. Console, Controller, and Other Hardware terms

General

game hardware	gēmu hādo	ゲームハード
(slang) game hardware	geha	ゲハ
used	chūko	中古
creator	mēkā	メーカー
first party	junseihin	純正品
genuine	junsei	純正
third party	sādo pātī	サードパーティー
third part product	sādo pātī seihin	製品
non-official product	hijunseihin	非純正品
product made by outside company	shagaihin	社外品
out-of-production	seisan shūryō	生産終了
discontinued	seisan chūshi	生産中止
it's cheap	anka da	安価だ
it's expensive	kōka da	高価だ
update	appudēto	アップデート
most recent	saishin	最新
VR	bui āru	VR
virtual reality	bācharu riariti	バーチャルリアリティ

Console terms

game console	gēmuki	ゲーム機
console	hontai	本体
(console name) version	...ban	...版
to turn on	kakeru	かける
startup sound	kidōon	起動音
startup screen	kidō gamen	起動画面
to turn off power	dengen o kiru	電源を切る
to restart	saikidō suru	再起動する
home console	katei yō gēmuki	家庭用ゲーム機
non-portable console	sueokiki	据え置き機
non-portable console	sueokigata gēmuki	据え置き型ゲーム機
home console games	kateiyō gē	家庭用ゲー
handheld system	keitaigata gēmuki	携帯型ゲーム機
compact	kompakuto	コンパクト
it fits in your pocket	poketto ni osamaru	ポケットに収まる
to carry	mochihakobu	持ち運ぶ
battery	denchi	電池
rechargeable battery	jūdenchi	充電池
running out of battery	denchigire	電池切れ
handheld game	keitaigata gēmu	携帯型ゲーム
8 bit	hachi bitto	８ビット

16 bit	jūroku bitto	１６ビット
32 bit	sanjūni bitto	32 ビット
32 bit console	sanjūni bitto gēmuki	32 ビットゲーム機
platform	purattofōmu	プラットフォーム
supported platforms	taiō purattofōmu	対応プラットフォーム
backward compatibility	kōhōgokansei	後方互換性
next generation	jisedai	次世代
to stand up a console	tate oku	縦置く
touchscreen	tacchi paneru	タッチパネル
sensitivity	kando	感度
to tap	tappu suru	タップする
to flick	furikku suru	フリックする
included in the package	dōkon	同梱

Cords

wall-outlet / plugin	konsento	コンセント
cable / cord	kēburu	ケーブル
extension cord	enchō kēburu	延長ケーブル
power supply	dengen kyōkyū	電源供給
AC adapter	ei shī adaputā	AC アダプター
power cord	dengen kēburu	電源ケーブル
coaxial cable	dōjiku kēburu	同軸ケーブル
ethernet cable	īsanetto	イーサネット

Controller Terms

controller	kontorōrā	コントローラー
wired	yūsen	有線
wireless	musen	無線
connection	setsuzoku	接続
battery	denchi	電池
rechargeable battery	jūdenchi	充電池
running out of battery	denchigire	電池切れ
lithium battery	richiumu denchi	リチウム電池
lithium-ion batter	richiumu ion denchi	リチウムイオン電池
Li-ion battery	ri ion denchi	Li-ion 電池
control scheme	sōsa hōhō	操作方法
to control	sōsa suru	操作する
not used to the controls	sōsa ni narete inai	操作に慣れていない
joystick	sutikku	スティック
to press (down)	osu	押す
move with	de sōsa	で操作
to move (the joystick)	ugokasu	動かす
to tilt	katamukeru	傾ける
D pad	jūji kī	十字キー
to press	osu	押す
press and hold	nagaoshi	長押し
to mash a button repeatedly	botan o renda suru	ボタンを連打する

A Button	ē botan	Aボタン
B Button	bī botan	Bボタン
X Button	ekkusu botan	Xボタン
Y Button	wai botan	Yボタン
with Y (button)	wai de	Yで
L Button	eru botan	Lボタン
R Button	āru botan	Rボタン
trigger	torigā	トリガー
Select Button	serekuto botan	ＳＥＬＥＣＴボタン
Start Button	sutāto botan	ＳＴＡＲＴボタン
with turbo function	rensha kinō tōsai	連射機能搭載
vibration	shindō	振動
see-through	sukeruton	スケルトン
see-through controller	sukeruton kontorōrā	スケルトンコントローラー
clear	kuria	クリア

Peripheral Terms

peripheral / accessories	shūhenkiki	周辺機器
made for (console name)	(hontai) senyō	（本体）専用
able to be used for (console name)	(hontai) taiō	（本体）対応
compatible	gokan	互換
fully compatible	kanzengokan	完全互換
memory card	memorīkādo	メモリーカード

capacity	yōryō	容量
headset	heddosetto	ヘッドセット
mic	maiku	マイク
strategy guide book	kōryakubon	攻略本
protective case	hogo kēsu	保護ケース
console skin	sukin shīru	スキンシール
screen protector	hogo firumu	保護フィルム
bubble	kihō	気泡
stand	sutando	スタンド
charging cord (for controller)	jūden kēburu	充電ケーブル
charger (for handheld)	充電器	充電器
to charge	jūden suru	充電する
battery pack	batterī pakku	バッテリーパック

Game Terms

video (game)	gēmu	ゲーム
physical version	pakkēji ban	パッケージ版
electronic version of a game	daunrōdoban	ダウンロード版
to release	hatsubai suru	発売する
release schedule	hatsubai sukejūru	発売スケジュール
launch-title	rōnchi taitoru	ローンチタイトル
pack (expansion)	pakku	パック
add-on pack	tsuika pakku	追加パック
add-on contents	tsuika kontentsu	追加コンテンツ
DLC	dī eru shī	DLC

previous game (in a series)	zensaku	前作
remake	rimeiku	リメイク
port	ishoku	移植
to port	ishoku suru	移植する
...was ported to (console)	(gēmuki) ni ishoku sareta	（ゲーム機）に移植された
(console) version	(gēmuki)ban	（ゲーム機）版
update	bājon appu	バージョンアップ
patch	pacchi	パッチ
bug fixes	bagu shūsei	バグ修正
disk	disuku	ディスク
cartridge	kasetto	カセット
cartridge	kātorijji	カートリッジ
to remove the cartridge	kātorijji o nuku	カートリッジを抜く
to insert the cartidge	kātorijji o sasu	カートリッジを差す
manual	kaisetsusho	解説書
manual	manyuaru	マニュアル
digital manual	denshi kaisetsusho	電子解説書
case	kēsu	ケース
to store (somewhere)	hokan suru	保管する
place where you store your games	hokan basho	保管場所

Display Terms

TV	terebi	テレビ
moniter	monitā	モニター
LCD	ekishō	液晶
LED	eru ī dī	LED
light emitting diode	hakkō daiodo	発光ダイオード
OLED	yūki eru	有機 EL
afterimage	zanzō	残像
pixel	pikuseru	ピクセル
4K	yon kē	4K
8K	hachi kē	8K
CRT	buraunkan	ブラウン管
monochrome	monokuro	モノクロ
the center of the screen	gamen chūō	画面中央
the bottom right of the screen	gamen migi shita	画面右下
the top left of the screen	gamen hidari ue	画面左上
to be cut off from the screen	gamen kara mikireru	画面から見切れる
to display	hyōji suru	表示する

Collecting Terms

collector	shūshūka	収集家
game collector	gēmu korekutā	ゲームコレクター
game collector	gēmu korekutā	ゲームコレクター

someone who likes having a lot of games	tsumi gēmā	積みゲーマー
to accumulate	tsumiageru	積み上げる
counter word for collections of games	maigumi	枚組
to collect	shūshū suru	収集する
collector's item	korekutāzu aitemu	コレクターズアイテム
special editon	tokubetsu ban	特別版
limited edition version	genteiban	限定版
limited edition	gentei	限定
artbook	ātobukku	アートブック
steelbook	suchīrubukku	スチールブック
retrogame	retorogēmu	レトロゲーム
the original version	orijinaruhan	オリジナル版
sealed box / unopened	mikaifūhin	未開封品
a hidden gem / masterpiece	kakureta meisaku	隠れた名作

Repair and Maintenance

General

to repair	naosu	直す
to repair	shūfuku	修復

to fix a controller	kontorōrā o naosu	コントローラーを直す
to fix it by yourself	jibun de naosu	自分で直す
to buy a new controller	kontorōrā o kainaosu	コントローラーを買い直す
to work	kiku	効く
it doesn't work	kikanai	効かない
to change the parts out	pātsu o kaeru	パーツを変える
spare (part, etc.)	supea	スペア
to break	kowareru	壊れる
defective product	furyōhin	不良品
customer support	kasutamā sapōto	カスタマーサポート
user support	yūza sapōto	ユーザサポート
warranty	hoshō	保証
within warranty	hoshōnai	保証内
to send in for repairs	shūri ni dasu	修理に出す
fragile	kowareyasui	壊れやすい
to break	koshō suru	故障する
solution (to something not working right)	kaiketsusaku	解決策
how to deal with something	taishohō	対処法
to replace something	kōkan suru	交換する
same model	dōkei	同型
battery replacement	denchi kōkan	電池交換

to replace the analog stick	anarogu sutikku o kōkan suru	アナログスティックを交換する

Maintenance

maintenance	mentenansu	メンテナンス
to disassemble something	bunkai suru	分解する
disassembly instructions	bunkai tejun	分解手順
to reassemble something	kumitatenaosu	組み立て直す
to put back together	kumitatenaosu	組み立て直す
how to put your controller back together	kontorōrā no kumitatekata	コントローラーの組み立て方
taking apart and cleaning	bunkai seisō	分解清掃
to restore	resutoa suru	レストアする
to clean (controller, console, etc.)	seisō suru	清掃する
to leave something alone	hōchi suru	放置する
to leave it alone for 24 hours	nijūyon jikan hōchi suru	24時間放置する
sticker	shīru	シール
sticker residue	shīru ato	シール跡
sticky	betabeta	ベタベタ

sticky residue	betabeta ato	ベタベタ跡
to clean the sticker residue	shīru ato o kirei ni suru	シール跡を綺麗にする
price sticker	nefuda	値札
to the remove price sticker	nefuda shīru o hagasu	値札シールを剥がす
dust	hokori	ホコリ
covered in dust	hokori mamire	ホコリまみれ
dirt	yogore	汚れ
grime	aka	垢
dirty	kitanai	汚い
corrosion (battery)	fushoku	腐食
the battery terminals are corroded	denchi tanshi ga fushoku shite ita	電池端子が腐食していた
rust	sabi	錆
stain	shimi	染み
discoloration	henshoku	変色
yellowing	kibami	黄ばみ
to yellow	kibamu	黄ばむ
to turn yellow	ōhen suru	黄変する
yellowed console	kibanda gēmuki	黄ばんだゲーム機
yellowed plastic	kibanda purasuchikku	黄ばんだプラスチック
to remove yellowing	kibami o toru	黄ばみを取る
to remove yellowing	kibami o otosu	黄ばみを落とす
to bleach	hyōhaku suru	漂白する

yellowed console	kibanda gēmuki	黄ばんだゲーム機
retrobright	retoroburaito	レトロブライト
hydrogen peroxide	kasankasuiso	過酸化水素
uv light	shigaisen	紫外線

Tools

screwdriver	doraibā	ドライバー
special screwdriver	tokushu na doraibā	特殊なドライバー
toothbrush	haburashi	歯ブラシ
cotton swab	membō	綿棒
to clean the contacts with a cotton swab	sesshokubu o membō de seisō suru	接触部を綿棒で清掃する
toothpick	tsumayōji	爪楊枝
isopropyl alcohol	isopuropiru arukōru	イソプロピルアルコール
concentration	nōdo	濃度
to use your nails	tsume o tsukau	爪を使う

Parts and Repair

crevice	sukima	隙間
parts	pātsu	パーツ
parts	buhin	部品
gyroscope	jairosukōpu	ジャイロスコープ
accelerometer	kasokudo sensa	加速度センサ

spring	bane	ばね
pad	paddo	パッド
battery cover	batterī kabā	バッテリーカバー
vent	tsūkikō	通気口
ventilation	kanki	換気
good ventilation	jōzu na kanki	上手な換気
PCB (printed circuit board)	purinto kiban	プリント基板
microfiber	maikurofaibā	マイクロファイバー
static electricity	seidenki	静電気
to get dry	kawaku	乾く
dry	kawaita	乾いた
the pins are dried	tanshi ga kawaita	端子が乾いた
dead battery	denchigire	電池切れ
soldering iron	handa gote	半田ごて
solder	handa	はんだ
contacts	setten	接点
contacts	sesshokubu	接触部
pins	tanshi	端子
terminals	tanshibu	端子部
to become wet	nurasu	濡らす
screws	neji	ネジ
to turn a screw	neji o mawasu	ネジを回す
outside	gaibu	外部
external screws	gaibu no neji	外部のネジ
inside / interior	naibu	内部
internal screws	naibu no neji	内部のネジ
to remove the screws	neji o toru	ネジを取る

to tighten (a screw)	shimeru	締める
to over tighten	shimesugiru	締めすぎる
stripped (screw hole)	tsubureta	潰れた
cartridge	kasetto	カセット
filthy cartridge	yogoreteru kasetto	汚れてるカセット
to be chipped / damaged	kakeru	欠ける
dent	hekomi	凹み
to degrade	rekka suru	劣化する
to come off	hazureru	外れる
the battery has degraded	batterī ga rekka shita	バッテリーが劣化した
broken controller	ikareta kontorōrā	イカれたコントローラー
my controller doesn't work	kontorōrā ga ugokanai	コントローラーが動かない
my controller broke	kontorōrā ga ikareta	コントローラーがイカれた
the joystick feels stuck	sutikku ga hikkakata kanji	スティックが引っかかった感じ
joystick moves on its own	sutikku ga katte ni ugoku	スティックが勝手に動く
callibrate	chōsei	調整
to not respond	han'nō shinai	反応しない
unresponsive	han'nō ga warui	反応が悪い
disk	disuku	ディスク
it can't read	yomikomenai	読み込めない

9. PC Gaming

General

computer	pasokon	パソコン
computer desk	pasokondesuku	パソコンデスク
PC gamer	pasokon gēmā	パソコンゲーマー
beautiful graphics	kirei na gurafikku	綺麗なグラフィック
realistic	riarisutikku	リアリスティック
precise movement	seimitsu na ugoki	精密な動き
restart	saikidō	再起動

Keyboard

keyboard	kībōdo	キーボード
gaming keyboard	gēmingu kībōdo	ゲーミングキーボード
high-performance	kōseinō	高性能
membrane keyboard	makugata kībōdo	膜型キーボード
membrane keyboard	memburen kībōdo	メンブレンキーボード
mechanical keyboard	mekanikaru kībōdo	メカニカルキーボード
tenkeyless	tenkī nashi	テンキーなし
tenkeyless	tenkīresu	テンキーレス

compact	kompakuto	コンパクト
quiet keyboard	seionsei ga takai kībōdo	静音性が高い
high durability	taikyūsei ga takai	耐久性が高い
cord / cable	kēburu	ケーブル
cable length	kēburu no nagasa	ケーブルの長さ
removable cable	chakudatsushiki kēburu	着脱式ケーブル
RGB backlit	āru jī bī bakkuraito tsuki	RGB バックライト付き
palm rest	pāmu resuto	パームレスト
linear	rinia	リニア
tactile	takutairu	タクタイル
clicky	kurikkī	クリッキー
actuation point	akuchuēshon pointo	アクチュエーションポイント

Keys

key	kī	キー
to type	utsu	打つ
to press down on a key	ōka suru	押下する
keystroke	daken	打鍵
sound it makes when you press	daken'on	打鍵音
key rollover	kī rōru ōbā	キーロールオーバー

NKRO	enu kī rōru ōbā	N キーロールオーバー
NKRO	enu kī rōru ōbā	NKRO
anti-ghosting	anchigōsuto	アンチゴースト
layout	hairetsu	配列
Japanese layout	nihongo hairetsu	日本語配列
English layout	eigo hairetsu	英語配列
key settings	kī settei	キー設定
programmable key	puroguramu kanō na kī	プログラム可能なキー
macro key	makuro kī	マクロキー
numeric keypad	tenkī	テンキー

Keycaps

keycap	kī kyappu	キーキャップ
mold	seikei	成型
to replace	kōkan suru	交換する
to customize	kasutamaizu suru	カスタマイズする
texture	shitsukan	質感
material (made of)	zaishitsu	材質
resin	jushi	樹脂
ABS resin	ē bī esu jushi	ABC 樹脂
PBT resin	pī bī tī jushi	PBT 樹脂
o-ring	ō ringu	O リング
doubleshot	daburu shotto	ダブルショット
doubleshot mold	nishoku seikei	二色成型
pudding	purin jō	プリン状

translucent	hantōmei	半透明
LED lighting	eru ī dī raitingu	LED ライティング
RGB lighting	āru jī bī raitingu	RGB ライティング

Switches

switch	jiku	軸
blue switch	aojiku	青軸
silver switch	ginjiku	銀軸
silver switch	shirubā jiku	シルバー軸
grey switch	gurē jiku	グレー軸
red switch	akajiku	赤軸
black switch	kurojiku	黒軸
brown switch	chajiku	茶軸
white switch	shirojiku	白軸
clear switch	sukeruton jiku	スケルトン軸

Mouse

mouse	mausu	マウス
gaming mouse	gēmingu mausu	ゲーミングマウス
wireless mouse	musen mausu	無線マウス
wired mouse	yūsen mausu	有線マウス
touch pad	tacchi paddo	タッチパッド
DPI	dī pī ai	DPI
mouse sensitivity	mausu kando	マウス感度
polling intervals / responsiveness	repōto rēto	レポートレート

tracking speed	torakkingu sokudo	トラッキング速度
lift off distance	rifuto ofu disutansu	リフトオフディスタンス
mouse sole	mauso sōru	マウスソール
mouse size	mausu no ōkisa	マウスの大きさ
mouse weight	mausu no omosa	マウスの重さ
you can adjust the weight	omosa ga chōsei dekiru	重さが調整できる
weight adjustable	omosa chōsei kanō	重さ調整可能
the mouse doesn't fit my hand	mausu ga te ni awanai	マウスが手に合わない
the mouse fits my hand	mausu ga te ni atte iru	マウスが手に合っている
texture	shitsukan	質感
glossy mouse	kōtaku ga aru mausu	光沢があるマウス
matte mouse	matto na mausu	マットなマウス
grip (not hand position)	gurippu	グリップ
side button (mouse)	saido botan	サイドボタン
scroll wheel	hoīru	ホイール
middle click	hoīru botan	ホイールボタン
tilt	chiruto	チルト
click	kurikku	クリック
to click	kurikku suru	クリックする
double click	daburu kurikku	ダブルクリック
left click	hidari kurikku	左クリック
right click	migi kurikku	右クリック
to move the mouse	mausu o ugokasu	マウスを動かす

to slide your mouse	mausu o suberaseru	マウスを滑らせる
cursor	kāsoru	カーソル
mouse pad	mausu paddo	マウスパッド

Monitor and Display

monitor	monitā	モニター
gaming monitor	gēmingu monitā	ゲーミングモニター
screen resolution	gamen kaizōdo	画面解像度
display method	hyōji hōhō	表示方法
to display	hyōji suru	表示する
pixel	pikuseru	ピクセル
LCD	ekishō disupurei	液晶ディスプレイ
monitor's response time	monitā no ōtō sokudo	モニターの応答速度
high speed	kōsoku	高速
low speed	teisoku	低速
afterimage	zanzō	残像
hertz	herutsu	Hz
60 Hz	rokujū herutsu	60Hz
144 Hz	hyaku yonjūyon herutsu	144Hz
Full HD	furu eichi dī	フル HD
built in speakers	supīkā tsuki	スピーカー付き
blue light filter	burūraito katto kinō	ブルーライトカット機能
the top left corner	hidari ue sumi	左上隅

the bottom left corner	hidari shita sumi	左下隅
the top right corner	migi ue sumi	右上隅
the bottom right corner	migi shita sumi	右下隅

Headphone

headphones	heddo fon	ヘッドフォン
gaming headset	gēmingu heddosetto	ゲーミングヘッドセット
mic	maiku	マイク
voice chat	boisu chatto	ボイスチャット
wired	yūsen	有線
wireless	musen	無線
fit of the headset	sōchakukan	装着感
noise cancelling	noizukyanseringu	ノイズキャンセリング
performance	seinō	性能
perfect performance	kampeki na seinō	完璧な性能
clear sound quality	kuria na onshitsu	クリアな音質
open headphones	kaihōgata heddohon	開放型ヘッドホン
comfortable	kaiteki	快適
sound quality	onshitsu	音質
to leak sound	oto ga soto ni moreru	音が外に漏れる

sound leakage	otomore	音漏れ
headband	heddobando	ヘッドバンド
adjustable length	nagasa chōsetsu	長さ調節
headband padding	heddobando no paddo	ヘッドバンドのパッド
ear pads	iyā paddo	イヤーパッド
frequency response	shūhasūtokusei	周波数特性
impedance	impīdansu	インピーダンス
sensitivity	kando	感度
driver	doraibā	ドライバー

Gaming Chair

gaming chair	gēmingu chea	ゲーミングチェア
fabric	kiji	生地
mesh	messhu	メッシュ
leather	rezā	レザー
breathability	tsūkisei	通気性
armrest	āmuresuto	アームレスト
seat height	zamen no takasa	座面の高さ
adjustable height	takasa chōsei dekiru	高さ調整できる
headrest	heddoresuto	ヘッドレスト
footrest	futtoresuto	フットレスト
rockable	rokkingu dekiru	ロッキングできる
reclinable	rikuraininingu dekiru	リクライニングできる
lumbar support	rambā sapōto	ランバーサポート

comfortable	kaiteki	快適
spacious	yuttari	ゆったり

Making Your Own

General

gaming PC	gēmingu pīshī	ゲーミング PC
desktop computer	sueokigata	据え置き型
home build	jisaku pasokon	自作パソコン
specs	shiyō / supekku	仕様 ／スペック
low specs	tei supekku	低スペック
benchmark	seinō hyōka	性能評価
high performance	seinō no takai	性能の高い
price	kakaku	価格
low priced	teikakaku	低価格
it cost hundreds of dollars	sūman'en suru	数万円する
it cost thousands of dollars	sūjūman'en suru	数十万円する
computer parts	pasokon no pātsu	パソコンのパーツ
model number	kataban	型番
creator of a part	mēkā	メーカー
compatible	gokansei ga aru	互換性がある
to install (a part)	toritsukeru	取り付け
to replace	kōkan suru	交換する
to turn off the power	dengen o kiru	電源を切る

to detach (a cable)	hazusu	外す
to remove (a part)	torihazusu	取り外す
to lift up	mochiageru	持ち上げる
to loosen	yurumeru	緩める
to assemble	kumitateru	組み立てる
grease	gurīsu	グリース
to grease	gurīsu o nuru	グリースを塗る
notch	kirikaki	切り欠き
to line up the notches	kirikaki o awaseru	切り欠きを合わせる
a gap	sukima	隙間
static electricity	seidenki	静電気
measures against static electricity	seidenki taisaku	静電気対策
pin	pin	ピン
number of pins	pin sū	ピン数
6 pin	roku pin	６ピン
jack	jakku	ジャック
plug	puragu	プラグ
to plug in	sasu	挿す
to be plugged-in	sasaru	挿さる
to unplug	nuku	抜く
to pull out	nuku	抜く
pin connector	pin konekuta	ピンコネクタ
receptacle	reseputakuru	レセプタクル
socket	soketto	ソケット
screw	neji	ネジ
to tighten	shimeru	締める
screwdriver	nejimawashi	ねじ回し

fastener	koteikingu	固定金具
to fasten	shimeru	締める
case	kēsu	ケース
airflow	eafurō	エアフロー
audio input port	ōdio nyūryoku pōto	オーディオ入力ポート
audio output port	ōdio shutsuryoku pōto	オーディオ出力ポート
bay	bei	ベイ
cooler	kūrā	クーラー
cooling system	kūringu shisutemu	クーリングシステム
cooling fan	reikyaku fan	冷却ファン
vent	tsūkikō	通気口
dust	hokori	ホコリ
canned air	ea dasutā	エアダスター
hard drive	hādodisuku doraibu	ハードディスクドライブ
memory capacity	memori yōryō	メモリ容量
transfer speed	tensōsokudo	転送速度
SDD	esu dī dī	SDD
HDD	eichi dī dī	HDD
memory / RAM	memorī	メモリー
slot number	surotto sū	スロット数
kilobyte	kirobaito	キロバイト
megabyte	megabaito	メガバイト
gigabyte	gigabaito	ギガバイト
terabyte	terabaito	テラバイト
motherboard	mazābōdo	マザーボード
motherboard	mazabo	マザボ

slot	surotto	スロット
socket	soketto	ソケット
battery	batterī	バッテリー
CPU	shī pī yū	CPU
GPU	jī pī yū	GPU
graphics card	gurafikku bōdo	グラフィックボード
graphics card	gurabo	グラボ
integrated (graphics card)	onbōdo	オンボード
sound card	saundokādo	サウンドカード
power supply	dengen kyōkyū	電源供給

Performance

specs	supekku	スペック
the computer's specs aren't enough	pī shī no supekku ga tarite inai	PC のスペックが足りていない
to lose stability	anteisei ga ochiru	安定性が落ちる
unstable	fuantei	不安定
visual lag	kakutsuku	カクつく
performance setting	seinō settei	性能設定
image quality	gashitsu settei	画質設定
to lower the image quality	gashitsu settei o sageru	画質設定を下げる
to lower the graphics setting	gurafikku settei o sageru	グラフィック設定を下げる
screen tearing	tiaringu	ティアリング

screen stuttering	sutattaringu	スタッタリング
refresh rate	rifuresshu rēto	リフレッシュレート
frame rate	furēmu rēto	フレームレート
stable frame rate	antei shita furēmurēto	安定したフレームレート
to lower your frame rate	furēmurēto o sageru	フレームレートを下げる
read and write rate	yomikaki sokudo	読み書き速度
system requirements	shisutemu yōken	システム要件
the game won't startup	gēmu ga kidō shinai	ゲームが起動しない
I can't install the game	gēmu o insutōru dekinai	ゲームをインストールできない
benchmark	benchimāku	ベンチマーク
overclock	ōbākurokku	オーバークロック
overclock	kurokku appu	クロックアップ
underclock	andākurokku	アンダークロック
recommended system requirements	suishōkankyō	推奨環境
anti-alias	anchieiriasu	アンチエイリアス
resolution	kaizōdo	解像度
brightness	akarusa	明るさ
volume	onryō	音量
frame rate	furēmu rēto	フレームレート
to crash	kurasshu suru	クラッシュする
improve performance	seinō kōjō	性能向上

Ping

ping	pingu chi	ping 値
to lower your ping	pingu chi o sageru	ping 値を下げる
the ideal ping	risōteki na pingu chi	理想的な ping 値
latency	reitenshi	レイテンシ
response time	hannō jikan	反応時間
stability	anteisei	安定性
transfer rate	tensō sokudo	転送速度
network	netowāku	ネットワーク
congestion	fukusō	輻輳
bits per second	bitto maibyō	ビット毎秒
lag	ragu	ラグ
laggy	hannō ga osoi	反応が遅い

Software

software	sofuto	ソフト
beta-software	bēta sofuto	ベータソフト
file	fairu	ファイル
vanilla	banira	バニラ
mod	kaizō	改造
modded version	kaizō ban	改造版
to mod	kaizō suru	改造する
to rewrite (code)	kakikaeru	書き換える

freeware	furī sofuto	フリーソフト
indie game	indī gēmu	インディーゲーム
open source	ōpunsōsu	オープンソース
unzip	kaitō	解凍
run (a program)	jikkō	実行
to install	insutōru suru	インストールする
to download	daunrōdo suru	ダウンロードする
downloading	daunrōdochū	ダウンロード中
complete	kanryō	完了
programmer	purogiramā	プログラマー
program	puroguramu	プログラム

10. RPG

General

role playing game	rōru pureingu gēmu	ロールプレイングゲーム
RPG	rō pure	ロープレ
turn-based	tān sei	ターン制
hack-and-slash	hakusura	ハクスラ
hack-and-slash elements	hakusura yōso	ハクスラ要素
RPG elements	āru pī jī yōso	RPG 要素
character creation	kyara meiku	キャラメイク

Battle

fighting	sentō	戦闘
battle	sentō	戦闘
to enter a fight	sentō ni hairu	戦闘に入る
before you enter a battle	sentō ni hairu mae ni	戦闘に入る前に
be defeated in battle	sentō ni haiboku suru	戦闘に敗北する
combat	sentō	戦闘
combat system	sentō shisutemu	戦闘システム
defeating enemies (in general)	teki o tōbatsu	敵を討伐

Encounters

encounter	enkaunto	エンカウント
encounter rate	enkaunto ritsu	エンカウント率
random encounter	randamu enkaunto	ランダムエンカウント
visible encounter (enemies visible on field)	shimboru enkaunto	シンボルエンカウント
sprite of enemy on field	shimboru	シンボル
to touch an enemy	teki ni fureru	敵に触れる
to start a battle	sentō o kaishi suru	戦闘を開始する
to approach	sekkin suru	接近する
the back (of character / enemy)	haimen	背面
preemptive attack	sensei kōgeki	先制攻撃
forced encounter	kyōsei enkaunto	強制エンカウント

Targeting

target	taishō	対象
unit	yunitto	ユニット
to a single unit	tantai ni	単体に
to all units	zentai ni	全体に
ally	mikata	味方
entire party	zen’in	全員

enemy	teki	敵
opponent	aite	相手
all enemies	teki zen'in	敵全員
area of affect	han'i ni	範囲に

Turn

turn	tān	ターン
5th turn	go tān me	5ターン目
maximum amount of turns	saidai tān	最大ターン

Actions

action	kōdō	行動
to attack	kōgeki suru	攻撃する
to defend / guard	bōgyo suru	防御する
movement	idō	移動
to run away	nigeru	逃げる

Types of Attacks

regular attack	tsūjō kōgeki	通常攻撃
chain attack	renzoku kōgeki	連続攻撃
counter attack	hangeki	反撃
AoE attack	han'i kōgeki	範囲攻撃

move / attack	waza	技
HP restoring attack	eichipī kaifuku kōgeki	HP 回復攻撃

Describing Attacks

physical attack	butsuri kōgeki	物理攻撃
defense ignoring attack	bōgyo mushi kōgeki	防御無視攻撃
magic attack	mahō kōgeki	魔法攻撃
AoE	han'i	範囲
to hit	ateru	当てる
to miss	misu suru	ミスする
to evade	kaihi suru	回避する
dodge / evasion	kaihi	回避

Magic

magic	mahō	魔法
spell	jumon	呪文
mana	mana	マナ
MP	emu pī	MP
to restore MP	emu pī o kaifuku	MP を回復
to convert into MP	emu pī ni henkan suru	MP に変換する
to cast	tonaeru	唱える
support magic	hojo mahō	補助魔法
recovery magic	kaifuku mahō	回復魔法

summon	shōkan	召喚
magic attack	mahō kōgeki	魔法攻撃
offensive spells	jumon kōgeki	呪文攻撃
to attack an enemy with magic	teki o mahō de kōgeki suru	敵を魔法で攻撃する
resistance	teikōryoku	抵抗力
immune to magic	mahō mukō	魔法無効
magic damage reflection	mahō damēji hansha	魔法ダメージ反射

Status Abnormalities

status abnormality	jōtai ijō	状態異常
bleed	shukketsu	出血
poison	doku	毒
poison damage	doku damēji	毒ダメージ
silence	chinmoku	沈黙
paralysis	mahi	麻痺
petrified	sekika	石化
sleep	suimin	睡眠
frozen	tōketsu	凍結
stun	sutan	スタン
confusion	konran	混乱

Buffs and Debuffs

buff	bafu	バフ

debuff	debafu	デバフ
base	kiso	基礎
base attack power	kiso kōgekiryoku	基礎攻撃力
max	saidai	最大
max HP	saidai eichipī	最大 HP
to increase	zōka suru	増加する
to raise	ageru	上げる
increased damage	damēji zōka	ダメージ増加
to raise attack power	kōgekiryoku o ageru	攻撃力を上げる
to decrease	genshō suru	減少する
decrease damage	damēji genshō	ダメージ減少
regen	kaifuku	回復
to absorb	kyūshū suru	吸収する
to ignore	mushi suru	無視する
to ignore defense	bōgyo mushi suru	防御無視する
damage nullification	damēji mukōka	ダメージ無効化
invincible	muteki	無敵

Damage

damage	damēji	ダメージ
damage taken	hi damēji	被ダメージ
when you take damage	hi damēji toki	被ダメージ時
amount of damage taken	hi damēji ryō	被ダメージ量
to deal additional damage	tsuika damēji o ataeru	追加ダメージを与える

critical hit	kuritikaruhitto	クリティカルヒット
critical hit rate	kuritikaru ritsu	クリティカル率
guaranteed (crit)	kanarazu	必ず
chip damage	kezuri	削り
physical damage	butsuri damēji	物理ダメージ
magic damage reflection	mahō damēji hansha	魔法ダメージ反射
elemental damage	zokusei damēji	属性ダメージ
water damage	mizuzokusei damēji	水属性ダメージ
damage reflection	damēji hansha	ダメージ反射
immune	mukō	無効
immune to physical attacks	butsuri mukō	物理無効
immune to magic	mahō mukō	魔法無効
to negate	mukōka suru	無効化する
to negate damage	damēji o mukōka suru	ダメージを無効化する
heal	kaifuku	回復
revive	sosei	蘇生

Elements

element	zokusei	属性
no element	muzokusei	無属性
fire	hizokusei	火属性
water	mizuzokusei	水属性
water attack	suizokusei no kōgeki	水属性の攻撃

ice	kōrizokusei	氷属性
to freeze something	kōrasu	凍らす
earth	tsuchizokusei	土属性
wind	kazezokusei	風属性
wind damage	kazezokusei damēji	風属性ダメージ
lightning	kaminarizokusei	雷属性
light	hikarizokusei	光属性
dark	yamizokusei	闇属性
elemental damage	zokusei damēji	属性ダメージ
water damage	mizuzokusei damēji	水属性ダメージ
resistance	taisei	耐性
element resistance	zokusei taisei	属性耐性
water resistance	mizu taisei	水耐性
fire resistance	hi taisei	火耐性
vulnerable to an element	zokusei ni yowai	属性に弱い
it's weak to water	mizuzokusei ni yowai	水属性に弱い

Other Fight Terms

hippai sentō 必敗戦闘
unwinnable fight, even if you win, a cutscene showing you losing appears
haiboku suru 敗北する
to be defeated
haiboku toshite atsukau 敗北として扱う
to be treated as though you were defeated

ittei tān made seizon suru 一定ターンまで生存する
to survive until a certain turn
make batoru 負けバトル
fight you are supposed to lose
tōsō dekinai batoru 逃走できないバトル
fight you can't run away from

Status

status screen	sutētasu gamen	ステータス画面
party	pāti	パーティ
entire party	pāti zentai	パーティ全体
order of party	tairetsu	隊列
leader	rīdā	リーダー
ally	mikata	味方
guest party member	gesuto kyara	ゲストキャラ
to join party	pāti kanyū suru	パーティ加入する
to leave (party)	ridatsu suru	離脱する
starting gear	shoki sōbi	初期装備

Stats

stats	sutētasu	ステータス
HP	eichipī	HP
MP	emu pī	MP
mana	mana	マナ
to use	shōhi suru	消費する

attack	kōgekiryoku	攻撃力
physical attack	butsuri kōgekiryoku	物理攻撃力
defense	bōgyo	防御
magic attack	mahō kōgekiryoku	魔法攻撃力
magic defense	mahō bōgyo	魔法防御
agility	binjōsei	敏捷性
accuracy	meichūritsu	命中率
evasion rate	kaihiritsu	回避率
luck	un	運
attack speed	kōgeki sokudo	攻撃速度
movement speed	idō sokudo	移動速度

Alignment

alignment	zokusei	属性
good alignment	zenzokusei	善属性
neutral alignment	chūyōzokusei	中庸属性
evil alignment	akuzokusei	悪属性

Skills

skill	sukiru	スキル
to use	shiyō suru	使用する
effect	kōka	効果
to be applied	noru	乗る
passive skill	passhibu sukiru	パッシブスキル
active skill	akutibu sukiru	アクティブスキル

time until you can use the skill again	sukiru saishiyō jikan	スキル再使用時間
cool down	kūru taimu	クールタイム
success rate	seikō ritsu	成功率
skill tree	sukiru tsurī	スキルツリー
skill points	sukiru pointo	スキルポイント
skill exp	sukiru keikenchi	スキル経験値
cost to learn	shūtoku hiyō	習得費用
remaining points (to spend on a skill etc.)	nokori pointo	残りポイント
level learned	shūtoku reberu	習得レベル
option	sentakushi	選択肢

Build

build	birudo	ビルド
to build	ikusei suru	育成する
to strengthen	kyōka suru	強化する
(status) points	pointo	ポイント
assigning status points	sute furi	ステ振り
to assign	furiwakeru	振り分ける
to reassign	furinaoshi	振りなおす
minmax	zen furi	全振り
to minmax	zen furi suru	全振りする
to specialize in	tokka suru	特化する
jack-of-all-trades	kyoku furi	極振り
balance	baransu	バランス

Common Classes

role	yakuwari	役割
role	rōru	ロール
class	kurasu	クラス
assist role	hojoyaku	補助役
offensive role	kōgeki yaku	攻撃役
healer	hīrā	ヒーラー
knight	kishi	騎士
soldier	senshi	戦士
archer	yumitsukai	弓使い
thief	tōzoku	盗賊
magician	mahōtsukai	魔法使い
mage	madōshi	魔導士
necromancer	shiryōtsukai	死霊使い
to summon	shōkan suru	召喚する

Equipment and Items

item level	aitemu reberu	アイテムレベル
to raise an item's level	aitemu reberu o ageru	アイテムレベルを上げる
recovery item	kaifuku aitemu	回復アイテム
potion	pōshon	ポーション
HP potion	eichi pī pōshon	HP ポーション
to restore HP	eichipī kaifuku suru	HP 回復する

MP potion	emu pī pōshon	MP ポーション
gear	bugu	武具
equipment	sōbi	装備
loadout	rōdoauto	ロードアウト
proficiency	juku rendo	熟練度
to raise proficiency	juku rendo o ageru	熟練度を上げる
weapon	buki	武器
sword	ken	剣
dagger	tanken	短剣
bow	yumi	弓
arrow	ya	矢
axe	ono	斧
spear	yari	槍
staff	tsue	杖
club	kombō	棍棒
cannon	taihō	大砲
class-specific	kurasu sen'yō	クラス専用
slot (weapon slots, etc.)	surotto	スロット
change weapons	buki henkō	武器変更
shield	tate	盾
armor	yoroi	鎧
armor	bōgu	防具
accessory	akusesarī	アクセサリー
ring	yubiwa	指輪
bracelet	udewa	腕輪
dark res	yami taisei	闇耐性
damage reflection	damēji hansha	ダメージ反射
max HP	saidai eichipī	最大 HP

Exploring, Quests, and Grinding

Exploring

exploration	tanken	探検
the field	fīrudo	フィールド
the item fell onto the field	aitemu ga fīrudo ni ochita	アイテムがフィールドに落ちた
to return to town	machi ni modoru	街に戻る
dungeon	danjon	ダンジョン
final dungeon	rasuto danjon	ラストダンジョン

Shops

shop	shoppu	ショップ
item shop	aitemu shoppu	アイテムショップ
merchant	shōnin	商人
item shop	dōguya	道具屋
weapons merchant	bukishōnin	武器商人
weapons shop	bukiya	武器屋
blacksmith	kajiya	鍛冶屋
armor shop	bōguya	防具屋
inn	yadoya	宿屋

Quests

event	ibento	イベント
quest	kuesuto	クエスト
to start a quest	kuesuto kaishi suru	クエスト開始する
quest starting location	kuesuto kaishi basho	クエスト開始場所
quest starting item	kuesuto kaishi aitemu	クエスト開始アイテム
to accept a quest	kuesuto o juchū suru	クエストを受注する
quest acceptance location	kuesuto juchū basho	クエスト受注場所
quest acceptance conditions	kuesuto juchū jōken	クエスト受注条件
quest info	kuesuto jōhō	クエスト情報
target monster	taishō monsutā	対象モンスター
recommended level (for a quest)	suishō reberu	推奨レベル
quest reward	kuesuto hōshū	クエスト報酬
to complete a quest	kuesuto kuria suru	クエストクリアする
main quest	mein kuesuto	メインクエスト
main story	mein sutōrī	メインストーリー
side quest	saido kuesuto	サイドクエスト
daily quest	yōbi kuesuto	曜日クエスト
gather quest	shūshū kuesuto	収集クエスト
kill quest	tōbatsu kuesuto	討伐クエスト
fetch quest	shutoku kuesuto	取得クエスト

quest chain	renzoku kuesuto	連続クエスト
quest chain	renzoku kue	連続クエ
sub quest	sabu kuesuto	サブクエスト
sub event	sabu ibento	サブイベント
limited time quest	kikangentei kuesuto	期間限定クエスト

Farming and Grinding

weak enemies	zako	雑魚
farming	kari	狩り
farming spot	kariba	狩場
exp farming	keikenchi gari	経験値狩り
gold farming	gōrudo gari	ゴールド狩り
leveling / grinding	reberingu	レベリング
to level / grind	reberingu suru	レベリングする
levelup (slang)	reberage	レベラゲ

Level and Exp

level	reberu	レベル
low level	hikui reberu	低いレベル
high level	takai reberu	高いレベル
level scaling	reberu sukēringu	レベルスケーリング
max level	saidai reberu	最大レベル
level cap	reberu kyappu	レベルキャップ
exp	keikenchi	経験値

exp bonus	keikenchi bōnasu	経験値ボーナス
to earn exp	keikenchi o kasegu	経験値を稼ぐ
to collect exp	keikenchi o kakutoku suru	経験値を獲得する
level up	reberu age	レベル上げ
levelup (slang)	reberage	レベラゲ
level up	reberuappu	レベルアップ
to level up	reberage suru	レベラゲする
when you level up	reberuappu toki	レベルアップ時
to rise (a stat)	jōshō suru	上昇する

RTS

real-time tactics	riaru taimu tatikusu	リアルタイムタクティクス
tactic	senjutsu	戦術
unit	yunitto	ユニット
attack power	kōgeki ryoku	攻撃力
speed	sokudo	速度
movement speed	idō sokudo	移動速度
upgrade	zōkyō	増強
upgrade	appugurēdo	アップグレード
resources	shigen	資源
wave	uēbu	ウエーブ
terrain effect	chikei kōka	地形効果
base	kichi	基地
construct a base	kichi o kensetsu suru	基地を建設する

tower defense	tawā difensu	タワーディフェンス
base	ryōchi	領地
tower	tawā	タワー
to invade	shin'nyū	侵入する
to call	shōkan suru	召喚する
to call back(troops)	shōkan suru	召還する
to place	haichi suru	配置する

Roguelike

roguelike game	rōgu raiku gēmu	ローグライクゲーム
adventurer	bōkensha	冒険者
dungeon	danjon	ダンジョン
randomly generated	randamu seisei	ランダム生成
item placement	aitemu haichi	アイテム配置
enemy placement	teki haichi	敵配置
tile	masu	マス
permadeath	kōkyūteki na shi	恒久的な死
food	shokuryō	食糧
empty stomach	kūfuku	空腹
to starve to death	gashi suru	餓死する

11. MMORPG

General

MMORPG	daikibo taninzū dōji sanka gata onrain āru pī jī	大規模多人数同時参加型オンライン RPG
multiplayer online rpg	fukusū pureiyā sanka gata onrain āru pī jī	複数プレイヤー参加型オンライン RPG
to log on	roguon	ログオン
log-in screen	rogu in gamen	ログイン画面
online	onrain	オンライン
online (slang)	on	オン
DC	setsudan	切断
server	sābā	サーバー
to select a server	sābā o sentaku suru	サーバーを選択する
maintenance	mentenansu	メンテナンス
instance	insutansu	インスタンス
pve	pī bui ī	PvE
pvp	pī bui pī	PvP
pvp	taijinsen	対人戦
account	akaunto	アカウント
account (slang)	aka	垢
avatar	abatā	アバター
account ban	akaban	アカ BAN
kick	kikku	kick

friends list	furendo risuto	フレンドリスト
register	tōroku suru	登録する
lobby	robī	ロビー
chat	chatto	チャット
irl	riaru	リアル
party chat	pāti chatto	パーティチャット
nearby chat	shūi cha	周囲チャ
nearby chat	shiro cha	白チャ
friend chat	fure cha	フレチャ
accidentally saying something in the wrong chat	gobaku	誤爆
player	pureiyā	プレイヤー
bot	botto	ボット
new player	shoshinsha	初心者
newb	zako	雑魚

Enemies and Combat

mob	mobu	モブ
weak enemy	zako	雑魚
group of enemies	shūdan	集団
monster	monsutā	モンスター
hostile	tekisei	適性
aggressive	akutibu	アクティブ
non aggressive	non akutibu	ノンアクティブ
to attack	kōgeki suru	攻撃する

to fight	tatakau	戦う
mechanic	mekanikusu	メカニクス
fight mechanics	sentō mekanikusu	戦闘メカニクス
loot	senrihin	戦利品
loot	rūto	ルート
drop	doroppu	ドロップ
boss monster	bosu monsutā	ボスモンスター
aggro	tage	タゲ
hate	heito	ヘイト
to take the aggro	tage o toru	タゲを取る
kiting	marason	マラソン
adds	zōen	増援
pull	tsuri	釣り
to pull	tsuru	釣る
to pull	hipparu	引っ張る
line of sight	shisen	視線
to detect	tanchi suru	探知する

Crowd Control

crowd control	kuraudo kontorōru	クラウドコントロール
AoE	han'i	範囲
damage over time	ittei jikan damēji	一定時間ダメージ
bleed	shukketsu	出血
active	akutibu	アクティブ
passive	passhibu	パッシブ
buff	bafu	バフ

heal over time	ittei jikan kaifuku	一定時間回復
debuff	debafu	デバフ
OP	tsuyosugiru	強すぎる
target	taishō	対象

Quest and Raid

event	ibento	イベント
event boss	ibento bosu	イベントボス
rewards	hōshū	報酬
limited time quest	kikangentei kuesuto	期間限定クエスト
daily quest	yōbi kuesuto	曜日クエスト
objective	mokuhyō	目標
main quest	mein kuesuto	メインクエスト
raid	reido	レイド
raid boss	reido bosu	レイドボス
dungeon	danjon	ダンジョン
dungeon farming	shūkai	周回
to clear	kuria suru	クリアする

Party

party	pāti	パーティ
clan	kuran	クラン
PUG	nora	野良
wipe	zenmetsu	全滅

member	kōseiin	構成員
to disband	kaisan suru	解散する
guild	girudo	ギルド
Guild vs Guild	jī bui jī	GvG

Roles

tank	kabe yaku	壁役
tank (shield)	tate yaku	盾役
support	shien yaku	支援役
support	sapōto yaku	サポート役
healer	hīrā yaku	ヒーラー役
dd	karyoku yaku	火力役
dd (attacker)	kōgeki yaku	攻撃役
dps (role)	dī pī esu yaku	DPS 役
to drop connection	ochiru	落ちる
to fall asleep and lose connection	neochi	寝落ち
to go AFK	riseki suru	離籍する
AFK	riseki chū	離籍中
idle	hōchi	放置

Character

character	kyara	キャラ
main	mochi kyara	持ちキャラ
alt	sabu kyara	サブキャラ

mule	sōko kyara	倉庫キャラ
class	kurasu	クラス
role	yakuwari	役割

Grinding and Farming

level	reberu	レベル
low level	hikui reberu	低いレベル
high level	takai reberu	高いレベル
level cap	reberu jōgen	レベル上限
max level	saidai reberu	最大レベル
exp	keikenchi	経験値
exp boost	keikenchi būsuto	経験値ブースト
carry	kyarī	キャリー
carrying a low level player to increase their level	pawāreberingu	パワーレベリング
carrying a low level player to increase their level	pawa rebe	パワレベ
carrying a low level player to increase their level	pī eru	PL
farming	rankaku	乱獲
farming	hori	掘り
camper	kyampā	キャンパー
farming group	giruhan	ギルハン
grinding	reberingu	レベリング

Stats

stats	sutētasu	ステータス
damage per second	byōkan damēji	秒間ダメージ
dps	dī pī esu	ｄｐｓ
dps (when used for damage in general)	karyoku	火力
damage	damēji	ダメージ
movement speed	idō sokudo	移動速度
attack speed	kōgeki sokudo	攻撃速度
I frame	muteki fure	無敵フレ
ability	nōryoku	能力
skill	sukiru	スキル
skill system	sukiru shisutemu	スキルシステム
time until you can use again	saishiyōjikan	再使用時間
cooldown	kūrutaimu	クールタイム
spec	furiwakeru	振り分ける
min-max	zenfuri	全振り
re-spec	furinaoshi	振りなおす

Items

item	aitemu	アイテム
special item	tokubetsu na aitemu	特別なアイテム
item exchange	aitemu kōkan	アイテム交換
ore	kōseki	鉱石

materials	shizai	資材
to not stack	sutakku shinai	スタックしない
gold	gōrudo	ゴールド
vendor	shōnin	商品
potion	pōshon	ポーション
recovery	kaifuku	回復
currency	tsūka	通貨
to trade	kōkan suru	交換する
cosmetic (armor)	sōshoku	装飾

Disliked Behavior

player kill	pureiyā kiru	プレイヤーキル
exp thief	keikenchi dorobō	経験値泥棒
loot ninja	rūtā	ルーター

12. Esports

General

tournament	taikai	大会
online tournament	onrain taikai	オンライン大会
eSports	ī supōtsu	e スポーツ
competitive game	taisen gēmu	対戦ゲーム
professional gamer	purogēmā	プロゲーマー
pro	puro	プロ
to make money with games	gēmu de okane o kasegu	ゲームでお金を稼ぐ
to become a pro gamer	purogēmā ni naru	プロゲーマーになる
sponsor	suponsā	スポンサー
to get sponsors	suponsā o kakutoku suru	スポンサーを獲得する
to belong to a team	chīmu ni shozoku suru	チームに所属する
to not belong to a team	chīmu ni shozoku shite inai	チームに所属していない
skill	giryō	技量
training	kunren	訓練
to train	kunren suru	訓練する
S Tier	esu ranku	S ランク
number one in world	zen'ichi	全一
best (user of a character)	zen'ichi (kyara)	全一（キャラ）

upset (low ranked beating higher ranked player)	bankuruwase	場狂わせ
to go to tournaments	taikai ni deru	大会に出る
to practice constantly	renshū o kasaneru	練習を重ねる

Common Esports Genres

fighting game	kakutō gēmu	格闘ゲーム
fighting game	kaku gē	格ゲー
FPS	efu pī esu	FPS
First-Person Shooter	fāsuto pāson shūtingu gēmu	ファーストパーソンシューティングゲーム
Third-Person Shooter	sādo pāson shūtingu	サードパーソンシューティング
MOBA	moba	MOBA

Signing up and Participating

tournament	taikai	大会
official tournament	kōshiki taikai	公式大会
sign-up page	shinseiyō pēji	申請用ページ
sign-up period	boshū kikan	募集期間
to seek participants for a tournament	sankasha o tsunoru	参加者を募る

entrant / participant	sankasha	参加者
maximum number of participants	saidai sanka ninzū	最大参加人数
to enter a tournament	taikai ni entorī suru	大会にエントリーする
spectator	kengaku	見学
number of applicants	ōbo sū	応募数
seeding	shīdo	シード
venue	kaijō	会場
tournament name	taikai na	大会名
event	ibento	イベント
entrance fee	sanka hi	参加費
date of event	kaisaibi	開催日
participation conditions	sanka jōken	参加条件
to administrate (the tournament)	unei suru	運営する
holding a tournament	kaisai suru	開催する
to cancel (a tournament)	chūshi suru	中止する
rule	rūru	ルール
tournament style	taikai keishiki	大会形式
single elimination	shinguru eriminēshon	シングルエリミネーション
double elimination	daburu iriminēshon	ダブルイリミネーション
number of sets	setto sū	セット数

ban (e.g. character)	kinshi	禁止
tournament schedule	taikai shinkō	大会進行
time schedule	taimu sukejūru	タイムスケジュール
start of the tournmanent		大会開始
check-in	chekku in	チェックイン
begin check-ins	chekku in kaishi	チェックイン開始
to confirm (you are at the tournament)	kakunin suru	確認する
check-in deadline	chekku in shimekiri	チェックイン〆切
to be finished with check-ins	chekku in sumaseru	チェックインを済ませる
deadline	shimekiri	〆切
begin preliminaries	yosen kaishi	予選開始
to begin your matches	taisen o hajimeru	対戦を始める
Quarter-Finals	junjunkesshō	準々決勝
Semi-Finals	junkesshō	準決勝
Grand Finals	kesshōsen	決勝戦
end of tournament	shūryō	終了

Results

tournament results	taikai seiseki	大会成績
results	seiseki	成績
ranking	rankingu	ランキング
champion	yūshōsha	優勝者
1st place	ichi'i	1位

winner / first place	yūshō	優勝
runner-up (second place)	junyūshō	準優勝
third place	san'i	3位
win rate	shōritsu	勝率
number of wins	kachi sū	勝ち数
prize money	shōkin	賞金
to earn prize money	shōkin o kasegu	賞金を稼ぐ
prize	shōhin	賞品
participation prize	sankashō	参加賞
preliminary prize	yosen shōhin	予選賞品
results of the set	taisen kekka	対戦結果
win	shōri	勝利
winner of the set	shōri shita hito	勝利した人
winner of the 2 rounds	nikaitomo shōri shita hito	二回とも勝利した人
to beat	taosu	倒す
win	kachi	勝ち
default win	fusenshō	不戦勝
lose	make	負け
to lose	makeru	負ける
disqualified	shikkaku	失格
loser (of a match)	haisha	敗者
winner (of a match)	shōsha	勝者

During the Tournament

match	taisen	対戦
VS	tai	対
during the match	taisenchū	対戦中
sweaty hands	tease	手汗
nerves	kinchō	緊張
to get nerves	kinchō suru	緊張する
to focus / concentrate	shūchū suru	集中する
(advice, etc.) coming from a pro	puro ni yoru	プロによる
to get emotional (salty)	kanjōteki ni naru	感情的になる
salty (feeling down after a match)	fukigen	不機嫌
salty (irritated)	iraira shiteru	イライラしてる
salty (angry)	buchigire	ブチギレ
opponent	aite	相手
game 1 / round 1	ikkaisen	一回戦
round	shiai	試合
set	setto	セット
1 set	ichi setto	1 セット
to take the set	setto senshu suru	セット先取する
best of 3	sanbon senshu	3 本先取
best of 5	gohon senshu	5 本先取
top rounds	honsen	本戦

round-robin	sōatari	総当たり
to report (your results)	hōkoku suru	報告する
the next match	jikai sen	次回戦
to move ahead	susumu	進む
rematch	saisen	再戦
to watch someone playing	kansen suru	観戦する
friendlies	furī taisen	フリー対戦
bracket	taisenhyō	対戦表
the brackets are up	taisenhyō ga happyō sareta	対戦表が発表された
main bracket (winners')	shōsha gawa	勝者側
losers' bracket	haisha gawa	敗者側
to advance to the next round	tsugi no raundo ni susumeru	次のラウンドに進める
preliminaries	yosen	予選
finals	kesshōsen	決勝戦
match	taisen	対戦
live broadcast	namachūkei	生中継
caster (commentator)	kyasutā	キャスター
analyst	anarisuto	アナリスト
player (*used mostly for esports)	senshu	選手

Talking About

beginner	shoshinsha	初心者
good	umai	うまい
a decent player	umai pureiyā	上手いプレイヤー
advanced player	jōkyūsha	上級者
tough (difficult)	kitsui	きつい
weak	yowai	弱い
weakness	yowami	弱み
strong	strong	強い
strength	tsuyomi	強み
rather strong	kanari tsuyoi	かなり強い
low risk (attack)	risuku ga hikui	リスクが低い
optimal	saiteki na	最適な
advantages	chōsho	長所
disadvantages	tansho	短所

Matchup

easy	raku	楽
50 / 50	gobun	五分
equal	gokaku	互角
disadvantage	furi	不利
advantage	yūri	有利
slight advantage	bi yūri	微有利

slight disadvantage	bi furi	微不利
patch	pacchi	パッチ
patch release	pacchi kōkai	パッチ公開
patch notes	pacchi nōto	パッチノート
to improve	kaizen suru	改善する
fix	shūsei	修正
bug fix	bagu shūsei	バグ修正
nerf	nāfu	ナーフ
buff	bafu	バフ
balancing	gēmu baransu	ゲームバランス

13. Fighting Games

General

fighting game	kakutō gēmu	格闘ゲーム
fighting game	kaku gē	格ゲー
fight stick	ake kon	アケコン
joystick	rebā	レバー
handplacement flat similar to a piano player's	piano oshi	ピアノ押し

Frames

frame unit	furēmu tan'i	フレーム単位
frame	furēmu	フレーム
frame	fure	フレ
startup	hassei	発生
active	jizoku	持続
recovery	kōchoku	硬直
total frames	zentai furēmu	全体フレーム
i frame	muteki furēmu	無敵フレーム
frame data	furēmu dēta	フレームデータ

Lag / Stun

lag / stun	kōchoku	硬直
lag	suki	隙
hit stun	hitto kōchoku	ヒット硬直
block stun	gādo kōchoku	ガード硬直
startup lag	mae suki	前隙
end lag	ato suki	後隙
landing lag	chakuchi kōchoku	着地硬直

Hitbox

collision box	hantei	判定
hitbox	kōgeki hantei	攻撃判定
hitbox duration	jizoku jikan	持続時間
hurtbox	kurai hantei	喰らい判定

Attacks

attack / move	waza	技
cheat move	chīto waza	チート技
strong moves	tsuyoi waza	強い技
weak moves	yowai waza	弱い技
ground attack	chijō kōgeki	地上攻撃
aerial attack	kūchū kōgeki	空中攻撃
anti-air	taikū	対空
punch	panchi	パンチ

kick	kikku	キック
projectile	tobidōgu	飛び道具
high	jōdan	上段
mid	chūdan	中段
low	gedan	下段
trade	aiuchi	相打ち
positioning	ichi	位置
charge	tame	溜め
crouching	shagami	しゃがみ
standing	tachi	立ち
to hit	ataru	当たる
easy to hit	atariyasui	当たりやすい
miss	misu	ミス
to miss	misuru	ミスる
telegraphed	yomiyasui	読みやすい
to avoid an attack	sakeru	避ける
to avoid a projectile	tobidōgu o sakeru	飛び道具を避ける
meter	gēji	ゲージ

Blocking

block	gādo	ガード
unblockable	gā fu	ガー不
block stun	gādo kōchoku	ガード硬直

Throwing

throw	nage	投げ
grab	tsukami	掴み

throw chain	nageren	投げ連
command grab	komando nage	コマンド投げ
command grab	koma nage	コマ投げ

General Combat

practice	jugyō	修行
training	rensei	錬成
teching	ukemi	受け身
playstyle	pureisutairu	プレイスタイル
button mashing randomly	reba gacha	レバガチャ
to offensively pressure	katameru	固める
read someone / reading	hitoyomi	人読み
read	yomi	読み
predict	sakiyomi	先読み
behavior / action	kōdō	行動
to capitalize on	ikasu	生かす
to totally commit to (a move, etc.)	ippentō	一辺倒
technique	tekunikku	テクニック
explanation (for how to do a technique)	kaisetsu	解説
defend against	fusegu	防ぐ
to check against	soshi	阻止
deals with	taiō suru	対応する

effective against	yūkō	有効
very effective	tokkō	特効
to connect (a hit)	awaseru	合わせる
options	sentakushi	選択肢
spacing	maai kanri	間合い管理
mindgame	shinrisen	心理戦
to react	hannō suru	反応する
punish	kakutei hangeki	確定反撃
safe	anzen	安全
pressure	puresshā	プレッシャー
to keep pressuring	puresshā o ataetsuzukeru	プレッシャーを与え続ける
to panic	aseru	あせる
mixup	yusaburi	揺さぶり
setup	setto purei	セットプレイ
baiting	tsuri	釣り
to interrupt	warikomi suru	割り込みする
zoning	machi	待ち
zoning character	machi kyara	待ちキャラ
camping	nige	逃げ
rushdown	tosshin	突進
edge of the screen	gamen hashi	画面端
wall	kabe	壁
to break	kowareru	壊れる
flowchart	sentaku	選択

Hitting

hit	hitto	ヒット
confirm	kakunin	確認
hit confirm	hitto kakunin	ヒット確認
invincible	muteki	無敵
meaty	omone	重ね
dodge	kaihi	回避
timing	taimingu	タイミング
cancel	kyanseru	キャンセル
cancellable	kyanseru kanō	キャンセル可能

The Neutral

neutral	nyūtoraru	ニュートラル
neutral game	nyūtoraru gēmu	ニュートラルゲーム
in the neutral	nyūtoraru jōtai	ニュートラル状態
to have the neutral (be in advantage)	tān	ターン
playing the neutral game	tān keizoku	ターン継続
neutral game	tachimawari	立ち回り
has a strong neutral	tachimawari ga tsuyoi	立ち回りが強い
poke	kensei	牽制
at a disadvantage	furi na jōkyo de	不利な状況で

at an advantage	yūri na jōkyo de	有利な状況で

Combo

combo	kombo	コンボ
to link	renkei suru	連係する
bread n butter combos	kihon kombo	基本コンボ
combo starter	kombo shidō	コンボ始動
combo breaking	abare	暴れ
combo breaker	abare waza	暴れ技
aerial combo	kūchū kombo	空中コンボ
juggling	otedama	お手玉
touch of death	sokushi	即死
infinite combo	eipa	永パ
infinite combo	eikyū kombo	永久コンボ
infinite combo	mugen kombo	無限コンボ
delay (a part of a combo)	direi	ディレイ
to pull off a combo	kombo o kansui suru	コンボを完遂する
to be able to do something without thinking (muscle memory)	muishiki ni dekiru	無意識にできる
in an actual match	jissen de	実戦で
Can you do it in an actually match?	Jissen de dekiru?	実戦でできる？
practical	jissenteki	実践的
reflexes	hanshashinkei	反射神経

Damage

damage	damēji	ダメージ
base damage	kiso damēji	基礎ダメージ
damage given	ataeru damēji ryō	与えるダメージ量
health	tairyoku	体力
healthbar	tairyoku gēji	体力ゲージ

Input and Command

input	nyūryoku	入力
to input	nyūryoku suru	入力する
to input a move	waza no nyūryoku o suru	技の入力をする
buffered input	senkō nyūryoku	先行入力
buffering	shikomi	仕込み
at the same time	dōji	同時
long press	nagaoshi	長押し
command	komando	コマンド

Movement

movement	dōsa	動作
to move	idō suru	移動する
to stand	tatsu	立つ
to crouch	shagamu	しゃがむ
to jump	jampu suru	ジャンプする

get up	okiagari	起き上がり
get up attack	okizeme	起き攻め

Character

character	kyara	キャラ
main	mochi kyara	持ちキャラ
main	mein kyara	メインキャラ
solo maining	tan kyara	単キャラ
secondary character	sabu kyara	サブキャラ
multi-main	ta kyara	多キャラ
character one is bad at	nigate kyara	苦手キャラ
labbing	kyara kaitaku	キャラ開拓
matchup	kādo	カード
bad matchup	furi kādo	不利カード
good matchup	yūri kādo	有利カード
counterpick	kabuse	被せ
to counterpick	kabuseru	かぶせる
techniques for fighting against a certain character	kyara taisaku	キャラ対策
tier list	daiaguramu	ダイアグラム
balance	baransu	バランス
high tier	jōi	上位
carried by a character	kyara kachi	キャラ勝ち
cheat character	chīto kyara	チートキャラ
mid tier	chūken	中堅

low tier	kai	下位
impossible matchup	tsumi	詰み
character matchup	kyara aishō	キャラ相性
character matchups chart	kyara aishō hyō	キャラ相性表
mirror match	mirā macchi	ミラーマッチ
ditto match	dō kyara taisen	同キャラ対戦
every character / any character	zen kyara	全キャラ
DLC character	dī eru shī kyara	DLC キャラ

14. FPS

General

FPS	efu pī esu	FPS
First-Person Shooter	fāsuto pāson shūtingu gēmu	ファーストパーソンシューティングゲーム
Third-Person Shooter	sādo pāson shūtingu gēmu	サードパーソンシューティングゲーム
beginner	shoshinsha	初心者
a decent player	umai pureiyā	上手いプレイヤー
advanced player	jōkyūsha	上級者

Aiming and Shooting

to aim at	nerau	狙う
aim	eimu	エイム
accurate aim	seikaku na eimu	正確なエイム
improve your aim	eimu jōtatsu	エイム上達
aiming skills	eimu nōryoku	エイム能力
aiming practice	eimu renshū	エイム練習
auto aim	ōto eimu	オートエイム
aim assist	eimu ashisuto	エイムアシスト
to miss a shot	hazusu	外す
to be bad at aiming	eimu ga nigate	エイムが苦手

to hit a shot	ateru	当てる
to hit	meichū suru	命中する
target	taishō	対象
headshot	heddoshotto	ヘッドショット
headshot	hessho	ヘッショ
no-scope	nōsukōpu	ノースコープ
quick scope	kuikku sukōpu	クイックスコープ
trickshot	torikkushotto	トリックショット
quickshot	kuikkushotto	クイックショット
gunfight	uchiai	撃ち合い
first shot	shodan	初弾
line of fire	shasen	射線
to break the line of fire	shasen o kiru	射線を切る
friendly fire	dōshi uchi	同士討ち
to shoot in short controlled bursts	tappu uchi	タップ撃ち
full auto	furuōto	フルオート
hip shooting	koshidame uchi	腰だめ撃ち
chip (damage)	kezuri	削り

Point of View

point of view	shiten	視点
to move your viewpoint	shiten o idō suru	視点を移動する
first-person view	ichininshō shiten	一人称視点
third person view	sanninshō shiten	三人称視点

camera	kamera	カメラ
sensitivity	kando	感度
camera sensitivity	kamera kando	カメラ感度
aim sensitivity	eimu kando	エイム感度
normal sensitivity	tsūjō kando	通常感度
high sensitivity	kōkando	高感度
low sensitivity	teikando	低感度

Combat

health	tairyoku	体力
regenerating HP	jidō kaifuku	自動回復
to knockdown someone	nokkudaun suru	ノックダウンする
to revive a teammate	mikata o sosei suru	味方を蘇生する
to get the kill	kiru o toru	キルを取る
killed	kiru sareta	キルされた
kill cam	kiru kame	キルカメ
kill streak	kiru sutorīku	キルストリーク
killing spree	renzoku kiru	連続キル
double kill	daburu kiru	ダブルキル
multi kill	maruchi kiru	マルチキル

Respawning

respawn	risupon	リスポン
respawn	fukkkatsu	復活
to respawn	fukkkatsu suru	復活する
respawn time	taiki jikan	待機時間
invulnerability period	muteki jikan	無敵時間
respawn point	risupōn chiten	リスポーン地点
spawn camper	risu imo	リス芋
spawn kill	risupōn kiru	リスポーンキール
spawn kill	risukiru	リスキル
spawn killing	risu kari	リス狩り

Tactics

tactic	senjutsu	戦術
enemy movement pattern	teki no idō patān	敵の移動パターン
enemy attack pattern	teki no kōgeki patān	敵の攻撃パターン
an advantageous situation	yūri na jōkyo	有利な状況
cover	kabā	カバー
a disadvantageous situation	furi na jōkyo	不利な状況

to find the enemy player	teki o mitsukeru	敵を見つける
to rush into the enemy	tobikomu	飛び込む
run and gun sniper	totsusuna	凸スナ
flanking	sokumenkōgeki	側面攻撃
flanking from behind	uratori	裏取り
blindspot	shikaku	死角
to shoot from an enemy's blindspot	teki no shikaku kara utsu	敵の死角から撃つ
to attack from an enemy's blindspot	teki no shikaku kara kōgeki suru	敵の死角から攻撃する
take the high grounds	ue o toru	上を取る
to ignore (the enemy)	surū suru	スルーする
to carry (weaker players)	kyarī suru	キャリーする
checking for nearby enemies	kuriaringu	クリアリング

Map

the map	mappu	マップ
to memorize the map	mappu o oboeru	マップを覚える
custom map	kasutamu mappu	カスタムマップ
to create a map	mappu o sakusei suru	マップを作成する
advantageous area	yūri na eria	有利なエリア

disadvantageous area	furi na eria	不利なエリア
advantageous position	kyō poji	強ポジ

Location

in front of you	shōmen de	正面で
the enemy right in front of you	mashōmen no teki	真正面の敵
behind	ushiro	後ろ
the enemy behind you	ushiro no teki	後ろの敵
the side	yoko	横
high ground	haigura	ハイグラ
to take the high ground	haigura o toru	ハイグラを取る
low ground	rōgura	ローグラ
to hide	kakureru	隠れる

Camping

camping / camper	imo	芋　／　イモ
to camp	imoru	芋る
Don't camp!	imoruna!	芋るな！
camping sniper	imomushi sunaipā	芋虫スナイパー
camping sniper	imosuna	芋砂
to camp with a sniper	sunaipā de imo suru	スナイパーで芋する

to lie prone	fuseru	伏せる
to snipe	sogeki suru	狙撃する
corner camping	kado machi	角待ち
to ambush	machibuseru	待ち伏せる
spawn camper	risu imo	リス芋
to spawn camp	risu imo suru	リス芋する
to hide	kakureru	隠れる
advantageous position (on the map)	kyō poji	強ポジ
to kill a camper	imo hori	芋掘り

Movement

to move	idō suru	移動する
move forward	zenshin suru	前進する
move backwards	kōtai suru	後退する
move left	hidari ni heikōidō suru	左に平行移動する
move right	migi ni heikōidō suru	右に平行移動する
to turn around	furimuku	振り向く
leaning	rīn	リーン
to run	hashiru	走る
to avoid (bullets, etc.)	kaihi suru	回避する
to slide	suraidingu suru	スライディングする
to crouch	shagamu	しゃがむ
shooting while crouching	shagami uchi	しゃがみ撃ち

to lie prone	fuseru	伏せる
side strafing while shooting	rerere uchi	レレレ撃ち
bunny hop	banī hoppu	バニーホップ
bunny hop	baniho	バニホ
parkour	parukūru	パルクール
wall running	wōru ran	ウォールラン
wall running	kabe hashiri	壁走り
to hide	kakureru	隠れる
to sprint	supurinto suru	スプリントする
to approach an enemy	teki ni chikazuku	敵に近づく

HUD

HUD	heddo appu disupurei	HUD
minimap	minimappu	ミニマップ
to check your position on the minimap	minimappu de ichi o kakunin suru	ミニマップで位置を確認する
to look at the minimap	minimappu o miru	ミニマップを見る
to be displayed on the minimap	minimappu jō ni hyōji sareru	ミニマップ上に表示される

Mission

stealth mission	suterusu ninmu	ステルス任務
escort mission	goei ninmu	護衛任務
to escort	goei suru	護衛する
combat mission	sentō ninmu	戦闘任務
rescue mission	kyūshutsu ninmu	救出任務
defense mission	bōei ninmu	防衛任務

Match Types

rank match	ranku macchi	ランクマッチ
free for all	furī fō ōru	フリーフォーオール
deathmatch	desumacchi	デスマッチ
time limit	seigenjikan	制限時間
team deathmatch	chīmu desumacchi	チームデスマッチ
capture the flag	hata tori kassen	旗取り合戦
king of the hill	jintori kassen	陣取り合戦

K/D and Score

K/D	kiru desu	K/D
K/D	kiru desu	キルデス
K/D	kiru desu	K/D
number of deaths	desu sū	デス数
number of kills	kiru sū	キル数
average...	heikin	平均
max...	saidai	最大
K/D ratio	kiru rēto	キルレート

K/D ratio (abbr)	kiru re	キルレ
K/D ratio	kiru desu hi	キルデス比
my K/D is high	kirure ga takai	キルレが高い
my K/D is low	kirure ga hikui	キルレが低い
to raise your K/D	kirure o ageru	キルレを上げる
score	sukoa	スコア
scoreboard	sukoabōdo	スコアボード
team score	chīmu sukoa	チームスコア

Cheating

no recoil	non rikoiru	ノンリコイル
wallhack	wōruhakku	ウォールハック
aimbot	eimu botto	エイムボット
auto-aim	ōto eimu	オートエイム
to use an aim bot	eimu botto o tsukau	エイムボットを使う
ghosting (cheat)	gōsutingu	ゴースティング

Weapons

General

weapon	buki	武器
to select	sentaku suru	選択する
to equip	sōbi suru	装備する
to change weapon	buki kirikaeru	武器切り替える
close ranged weapon	kinkyori buki	近距離武器

mid ranged weapon	chūkyori buki	中距離武器
long ranged weapon	enkyori buki	遠距離武器
close range combat	kinkyori sen	近距離戦
mid range combat	chūkyori sen	中距離戦
long range combat	enkyori sen	遠距離戦

Guns

gun	jū	銃
handgun	handogan	ハンドガン
pistol	pisutoru	ピストル
magnum	magunamu	マグナム
revolver	riborubā	リボルバー
shotgun	shottogan	ショットガン
12 gauge	jūni gēji	12 ゲージ
machine gun	mashingan	マシンガン
machine gun	kikanjū	機関銃
light machine gun	keiki kanjū	軽機関銃
submachine gun	tankikanjū	短機関銃
submachine gun	sabumashingan	サブマシンガン
rifle	shōjū	小銃
sniper rifle	sogekijū	狙撃銃
sniper rifle	sunaipā raifuru	スナイパーライフル
sniper	suna	スナ
sniper	suna	砂
sniper killing spree	ren suna	連砂

zoom	zūmu ritsu	ズーム率
2x	nibai	2倍
minigun	minigan	ミニガン
bow and arrow	yumiya	弓矢

Close Range

machete	machetto	マチェット
chainsaw	chēnsō	チェーンソー
brass knuckles	merikensakku	メリケンサック
flashlight	furasshuraito	フラッシュライト
crowbar	bāru	バール
unarmed	sude	素手

Supplies

ammo	dan'yaku	弾薬
remaining ammo	zandansū	残弾数
infinite ammunition	mugen ni uteru	無限に撃てる
armor piercing ammo	tekkōdan	徹甲弾

Stats and Parts

gun accuracy	meichūseido	命中精度
recoil	rikoiru	リコイル

recoil	handō	反動
rate of fire	rensha sokudo	連射速度
accuracy	meichūritsu	命中率
range	shatei	射程
attack power	kōgekiryoku	攻撃力
fire rate	rensharyoku	連射力
weapon slot	buki surotto	武器スロット
clip	kurippu	クリップ
magazine	dansō	弾倉
magazine	magajin	マガジン
amount of bullets magazine can have	sōdansū	装弾数
red dot sight	dotto saito	ドットサイト
night vision	naitobijon	ナイトビジョン
silencer	sairensā	サイレンサー
scope	sukōpu	スコープ

Actions

to shoot a weapon	hassha suru	発射する
to reload	rirōdo suru	リロードする
to change weapons	buki henkō	武器変更
to equip	sōbi suru	装備する
to aim	nerau	狙う
aim	nerai	狙い
to target (slang)	tageru	タゲる
crosshair	kurosuhea	クロスヘア
reticle	retikuru	レティクル

reticle / sights	shōjun	照準
friendly fire	dōshi uchi	同士打ち
hip fire	koshi uchi	腰撃ち
bullets	tama	弾
to take damage	damēji o ukeru	ダメージを受ける

Explosives

bomb	bakudan	爆弾
to be blown up	bakushi	爆死
the blast	bakufū	爆風
to get caught in the blast	bakufū ni makikomareru	爆風に巻き込まれ
hand grenade	shuryūdan	手榴弾
to throw	nageru	投げる
sticky grenade	nenchaku bakudan	粘着爆弾
smoke grenade	hatsuen shuryūdan	発煙手榴弾
landmine	jirai	地雷
C4	shī yon	C4
to plant	shikakeru	仕掛ける
detonate	kibaku suru	起爆する
dynamite	dainamaito	ダイナマイト
explosion	bakuhatsu	爆発
Molotov cocktail	kaenbin	火炎瓶
flamethrower	kaenhōshaki	火炎放射器
flashbang	furasshuban	フラッシュバン
RPG	āru pī jī	RPG

rocket	roketto	ロケット
grenade launcher	tekidantō	擲弾筒

Misc

loadout	rōdoauto	ロードアウト
n00b	zako	雑魚
lobby	robī	ロビー
tank	sensha	戦車

15. MOBA

General

MOBA	moba	MOBA
rank match	ranku macchi	ランクマッチ
early game	joban	序盤
mid-game	chūban	中盤
late game	shūban	終盤

Lane

lane	rēn	レーン
laning	rēningu	レーニング
lane control	rēn kontorōru	レーンコントロール
laner	rēnā	レーナー
off lane	rēnigai	レーン以外
top lane	toppu rēn	トップレーン
top path	ue no mich	上の道
mid lane	middo rēn	ミッドレーン
middle path	chūō no michi	中央の道
bottom lane	botomu rēn	ボトムレーン
bottom path	shita no michi	下の道
short lane	shōto rēn	ショートレーン
long lane	rongu rēn	ロングレーン
farm lane	fāmu rēn	ファームレーン
bot lane	botto rēn	ボットレーン
solo laning	soro rēn	ソロレーン

jungle	janguru	ジャングル

Creeps

creeps	kurīpu	クリープ
enemy creep	teki kurīpu	敵クリープ
neutral creep	chūritsu kurīpu	中立クリープ
allied creep	mikata kurīpu	味方クリープ
minion	minion	ミニオン
field of view	shiya	視野
farming	fāmu	ファーム
to farm	fāmu suru	ファームする
to kill (a creep / enemy player)	taosu	倒す
stack	sutakku	スタック
to stack	chōfuku suru	重複する
to stack	sutakku suru	スタックする
to accumulate stacks	sutakku o tameru	スタックを溜める
1 stack	ichi sutakku	1スタック
number of stacks	sutakku sū	スタック数
to earn gold	gōrudo o kasegu	ゴールドを稼ぐ
growth	seichō	成長
to hinder	bōgai suru	妨害する

Map and Positioning

the map	mappu	マップ
corner (of the map)	sumi	隅
bottom left	hidari shita	左下
bottom right	migi shita	右下
top left	hidari ue	左上
top right	migi ue	右上
position	ichi	位置
to spawn	supōn suru	スポーんする
respawn	fukkatsu	復活
to warp	wāpu suru	ワープする
to teleport	terepōto suru	テレポートする

Combat

unit	yunitto	ユニット
team	chīmu	チーム
ally	mikata	味方
enemy	teki	敵
low HP	tei eichi pī	低 HP
field of vision	shikai	視界
the opponents field of vision	aite no shikai	相手の視界
target	taishō	対象
near the target	taishō no shūi	対象の周囲

to overlook something	miotosu	見落とす
skill	sukiru	スキル
passive skill	passhibu sukiru	パッシブスキル
active skill	akutibu sukiru	アクティブスキル
ability	abiriti	アビリティ
passive ability	passhibu abiriti	パッシブアビリティ

Attacks

attack	kōgeki	攻撃
ult (ultimate)	uruto	ウルト
regular / standard attack	tsūjō kōgeki	通常攻撃
ranged attack	enkaku kōgeki	遠隔攻撃
effect	kōka	効果
gank	ganku	ガンク
surprise attack	kishū	奇襲
AoE	han'i	範囲
area of effect attack	han'i kōgeki	範囲攻撃
within range (of an AoE)	han'i nai	範囲内
melee / short ranged	kinkyori	近距離
melee attack	kinsetsu kōgeki	近接攻撃
ranged	enkyori	遠距離
move / attack	waza	技
spells	jumon	呪文
to use continuously	renpatsu suru	連発する

to summon	shōkan suru	召喚する
cooldown time	kūrutaimu	クールタイム
projectile	tobidōgu	飛び道具
HP absorption	eichi pī kyūshū	HP 吸収
stun	sutan	スタン

Damage

damage	damēji	ダメージ
to inflict damage	damēji o ataeru	ダメージを与える
to chip (damage)	kezuru	削る
invulnerable	muteki	無敵
to avoid (e.g. an attack)	kaihi suru	回避する
heal	hīru	ヒール
regenerate	kaifuku	回復
critical	kuritikaru	クリティカル
chance of occurring	hassei kakuritsu	発生確率
armor	āmā	アーマー

Teamwork

all members (of a team)	zen'in	全員
synergy (between teammates)	aishō	相性
an assist	ashisuto	アシスト
support	sapōto	サポート

to receive support	sapōto shite morau	サポートして貰う
team	chīmu	チーム
heal	hīru	ヒール
group combat	shūdansen	集団戦
one on one	ichi tai ichi	1 対 1
two on one	ni tai ichi	2 対 1
two on two	ni tai ni	2 対 2
five on five	go tai go	5 対 5
friendly unit	mikata yunitto	味方ユニット
nearby	shūi no	周囲の
nearby enemy unit	shūi no teki yunitto	周囲の敵ユニット
nearby allies	shūi no mikata	周囲の味方

Stats

stats	sutētasu	ステータス
HP	eichi pī	HP
max HP	saidai eichi pī	最大 HP
mana	mana	マナ
consumption	shōhi	消費
max mana	saidai mana	最大マナ
magic	mahō	魔法
range	shatei	射程
base	kiso	基礎
base attack speed	kiso kōgeki sokudo	基礎攻撃速度
attack power	kōgeki ryoku	攻撃力
attack range	kōgeki shatei	攻撃射程
base damage	kihon damēji	基本ダメージ

damage per second	byōkan damēji	秒間ダメージ
dps	dī pī esu	ｄｐｓ
movement speed	idō sokudo	移動速度
defense	bōgyo	防御
resistance	taisei	耐性
magic res	mahō taisei	魔法耐性
cooldown time	kūrutaimu	クールタイム

Buffs and Debuffs

buffs	bafu	バフ
aura	ōra	オーラ
to give	hanatsu	放つ
debuffs	debafu	デバフ
to remove	kesu	消す
effect	kōka	効果
duration of an effect	kōka jikan	効果時間
seconds	byō	秒
5 seconds	go byō	5 秒
every second	mai byō	毎秒
max	saidai	最大
to increase	zōka suru	増加する
cooldown increase	kūrutaimu zōka	クールタイム増加
to deal additional damage	tsuika damēji o ataeru	追加ダメージを与える
to raise	jōshō saseru	上昇させる
to raise defense	bōgyoryoku o jōshō saseru	防御力を上昇させる

amount of increase	jōshō ryō	上昇量
to decrease	genshō saseru	減少させる
cooldown reduction	kūrutaimu genshō	クールタイム減少
to reduce	teika suru	低下する

Level and Build

level	reberu	レベル
low level	hikui reberu	低いレベル
high level	takai reberu	高いレベル
max level	saidai reberu	最大レベル
experience points	keikenchi	経験値
to upgrade	appugurēdo suru	アップグレードする
strong point	tokui	得意
high attack	takai kōgekiryoku	高い攻撃力
role	yakuwari	役割
carry	kyarī	キャリー
tank	tanku	タンク
healer	hīrā	ヒーラー
support	hojoyaku	補助役
low attack	hikui kōgekiryoku	低い攻撃力
support	sapōto	サポート
jungler	jangurā	ジャングラー
build	birudo	ビルド
tank build	tanku birudo	タンクビルド
recommended build	osusume birudo	おすすめビルド
best build	saikyō birudo	最強ビルド

skill point	sukiru pointo	スキルポイント
to unlock	rokku o kaijjo	ロックを解除
to select	sentaku suru	選択する

Bases and Towers

tower	tawā	タワー
tier 1	fāsuto	ファースト
tier 2	sekando	セカンド
tier 3	sādo	サード
enemy tower	teki tawā	敵タワー
tower	kyoten	拠点
building	tatemono	建物
tier (of building)	dan	段
to destroy a building	tatemono o hakai suru	建物を破壊する
base / camp (area surround the building)	kichi	基地
camp	kyampu	キャンプ
enemy base	tekijin	敵陣
enemy base (the area surround the building)	teki kichi	敵基地
to invade the enemy base	teki kichi ni semekomu	敵基地に攻め込む
base (the building itself)	honkyochi	本拠地
to destroy the enemy base	teki honkyochi o hakai suru	敵本拠地を破壊する

Items and Shopping

shop	shoppu	ショップ
shop menu	shoppu menyū	ショップメニュー
item shop	aitemu shoppu	アイテムショップ
to buy	kōnyū suru	購入する
your current gold	shojikin	所持金
gold	gōrudo	ゴールド
recovery item	kaifuku aitemu	回復アイテム
to restore (health)	kaifuku suru	回復する
item	aitemu	アイテム
powerful item	kyōryoku na aitemu	強力なアイテム
item effect	aitemu no kōka	アイテムの効果

16. Arcade

At the Arcade

arcade	gēmu sentā	ゲームセンター
arcade	gēsen	ゲーセン
prize	puraizu	プライズ
arcade game	ākēdo gēmu	アーケードゲーム
arcade version	ākēdoban	アーケード版
coin	koin	コイン
insert coin	koin tōnyū	コイン投入
coin slot	koin tōnyū guchi	コイン投入口
credit	kurejitto	クレジット
token	tōkun	トークン

Common Types

dot eater game	dotto īto	ドットイート
dot	dotto	ドット
to collect	kaishū suru	回収する
racing game	rēsu gēmu	レースゲーム
fighting game	kakugē	格ゲー
beat'em up	berutosukurōru	ベルトスクロール
beat'em up	berusuku	ベルスク
shooter	shūtingu gata	シューティングゲーム

verticle scroller	tate shū	縦シュー
side scroller	yoko shū	横シュー
rail shooter game	gan shūtingu gēmu	ガンシューティングゲーム
music game / rhythm game	ongaku gēmu	音楽ゲーム
music / rhythm game	otogē	音ゲー
rhythm game	rizumu gē	リズムゲー

Life and Game Over

game over	gēmu ōbā	ゲームオーバー
continue	kontinyū	コンティニュー
continue screen	kontinyū gamen	コンティニュー画面
restart	sai sutāto	再スタート
life	ki	機
remaining lives	zanki	残機
to use a life	ki o shōhi suru	機を消費する
to lose a life	misu suru	ミスする

Stage

level / stage	sutēji	ステージ
beginning of the level	sutēji kaishi	ステージ開始
bonus stage	bōnasu sutēji	ボーナスステージ

Enemies

enemy	teki	敵
tough enemy	nanteki	難敵
weak enemies	zako	ザコ
boss	bosu	ボス
mid game boss	chū bosu	中ボス
final boss	saishū bosu	最終ボス

Score

score	tokuten	得点
score	sukoa	スコア
score display	tokuten hyōji	得点表示
high score	kōtokuten	高得点
point	ten	点
bonus point	bōnasu ten	ボーナス点

Time Limit

time limit	seigenjikan	制限時間
within the time limit	seigenjikan nai	制限時間内
time-out	jikangire	時間切れ

Other

power up	pawā appu	パワーアップ
sound effect	kōkaon	効果音
P1	pī wan	P1
P2	pī tsū	P2
simultaneous two player	futari dōji purei	2 人同時プレイ

Cabinets

circuit board	kiban	基盤
cabinet	kyōtai	筐体
arcade cabinet	ākēdo kyōtai	アーケード筐体
upright	appuraito kyōtai	アップライト筐体
mini cabinet	miniappuraito kyōtai	ミニアップライト筐体
environmental	ōgata kyōtai	大型筐体
environmental	senyō kyōtai	専用筐体
deluxe cabinet	taikan kyōtai	体感筐体
table cabinet	tēburu kyōtai	テーブル筐体
countertop cabinet	kauntātoppu kyōtai	カウンタートップ筐体
candy cabinet	hanyō kyōtai	汎用筐体
hardware limitations	hādo seiyaku	ハード制約

Screen

screen	gamen	画面
display	hyōji	表示
color	karā	カラー
monochrome	monokuro	モノクロ
overlay	iro serohan	色セロハン

Control Panel

control panel	kontorōru paneru	コントロールパネル
control panel	kompane	コンパネ
joystick	rebā	レバー
button	botan	ボタン
pause button	pōzu botan	ポーズボタン
select button	serekuto botan	セレクトボタン
start button	sutāto botan	スタートボタン
attack button	kōgeki botan	攻撃ボタン
jump button	jampu botan	ジャンプボタン
shoot button	hassha botan	発射ボタン

Beat 'em Up

side scrolling beat'em up	berutosukurōru	ベルトスクロール
beat'em up	berusuku	ベルスク
to scroll	sukurōru suru	スクロールする
to progress	shinkō suru	進行する
area	eria	エリア
to move to the next area	tsugi no eria ni susumu	次のエリアに進む
to defeat the enemies	teki o taosu	敵を倒す
to defeat all the on-screen enemies	teki o zenmetsu suru	敵を全滅する
bonus stage	bōnasu sutēji	ボーナスステージ
weapon	buki	武器
item	aitemu	アイテム
to pick up	hirou	拾う

Shooter

shooter	shūtingu gata	シューティングゲーム
to shot	utsu	撃つ
to aim	nerau	狙う
bullet	tama	弾

enemy bullet	tekidan	敵弾
number of shots	hatsu	発
2 shots	nihatsu	２発
bonus points	bōnasu ten	ボーナス点

Rail Shooter

rail shooter game	gan shūtingu gēmu	ガンシューティングゲーム
rail shooter	ganshū	ガンシュー
rail (movement)	rēru shiki	レール式
gun controller	gan kon	ガンコン
stage	sutēji	ステージ
to fail	shippai suru	失敗する
mission	ninmu	任務
to fail a mission	ninmu ga shippai suru	任務が失敗する
mission failed	ninmu shippai	任務失敗
to reload	rirōdo suru	リロードする
offscreen	gamengai	画面外
shoot offscreen	gamengai o utsu	画面外を撃つ
aim offscreen	gamengai ni jū o mukeru	画面外に銃を向ける
to aim	nerau	狙う
to hit (successful shot)	ataru	当たる
weak spot	jakuten	弱点
aim settings	shōjun settei	照準設定

civilian	ippanjin	一般人
penalty	penarutī	ペナルティー
to take damage	damēji o ukeru	ダメージを受ける
health kit	kusuri bako	薬箱
enemy fire	teki no shageki	敵の射撃
to be hit by the enemy	teki ni utareru	敵に撃たれる
to continue	kontinyū suru	コンティニューする
credit	kurejitto	クレジット
stage select	sutēji sentaku	ステージ選択
to return to stage select	sutēji sentaku ni modoru	ステージ選択に戻る

Rhythm Game

music game / rhythm game	ongaku gēmu	音楽ゲーム
music / rhythm game	otogē	音ゲー
rhythm game	rizumu gē	リズムゲー
song select screen	senkyoku gamen	選曲画面
to select a song	kyoku sentaku suru	曲選択する
track / song	kyoku	曲
random	omakse	おまかせ
to fail (a song)	shippai suru	失敗する
perfect score	manten	満点
new song	shinkyoku	新曲
hidden song	kakushi kyoku	隠し曲
note	nōto	ノート

beginning (of a note)	shiten	始点
end (of a note)	shūten	終点
to keep pressing	oshi tsuzukeru	押し続ける
to let go of (the button)	hanasu	放す
to miss (a note)	misu suru	ミスする
timing	taimingu	タイミング
miss	misu	ミス
combo	kombo	コンボ
to mess up a combo	kombo ga kireru	コンボが切れる
accuracy	seikaku	正確
good	ii	良
ok	ka	可
bad	fuka	不可

17. Side Scrolling Shooter

General

sidescrolling shooter	yoko sukurōru shūtingu	横スクロールシューティング
verticle scroller	tate shū	縦シュー
verticle scrolling shooter	tate sukurōru shūtingu	縦スクロールシューティング
side scroller	yoko shū	横シュー
side view	saidobyū	サイドビュー
top view	toppubyū	トップビュー
to scroll	sukurōru suru	スクロールする
to scroll from left to right	hidari kara migi e sukurōru suru	左から右へスクロールする
to stop scrolling	sukurōru ga tomaru	スクロールが止まる
counter stop (reaching the limit of a score, etc)	kansuto	カンスト

Obstacles

obstacle	shōgaibutsu	障害物

to dodge	kaihi suru	回避する
falling objects	rakkabutsu	落下物
enemy bullets	teki dan	敵弾
avoid enemy bullets	teki dan o sakeru	敵弾を避ける
to thread between attacks	nuu	縫う
safe spot	anchi	安地
wall	kabe	壁
the terrain	chikei	地形
indestructible	hakai funō	破壊不能
destroyable	hakai kanō	破壊可能
debris	hahen	破片
collision	shōtotsu	衝突
to collide	shōtotsu suru	衝突する
to crash into the terrain	chikei ni shōtotsu suru	地形に衝突する
to run into (an obstacle)	butsukaru	ぶつかる

Powerups and Types of Weapons

powerup	pawā appu	パワーアップ
equip a powerup	pawā appu o sōbi suru	パワーアップを装備する
to destroy all enemies	teki o zenmetsu suru	敵を全滅する
two directional	niren	二連
three directional	sanren	三連
shot	shotto	ショット

charge	tame uchi	溜め撃ち
laser	rēzā	レーザー
ability to penetrate (through an enemy)	kantsūryoku	貫通力
missile	misairu	ミサイル
to shoot a missile	misairu o hassha suru	ミサイルを発射する
wave	uēbu	ウエーブ
regular bullets	tsūjōdan	通常弾
rate of fire	renshasei	連射性
bomb	bomu	ボム
blast	bakufū	爆風

Movement

your ship	jiki	自機
movement	idō	移動
to move	idō suru	移動する
movement speed	idō sokudo	移動速度
increase your movement speed	idō sokudo o agaru	移動速度を上がる
forward	zenpō	前方
diagonally	naname	斜め
to move diagonally up	naname ue ni idō suru	斜め上に移動する
below	shimo ni	下に
above	ue ni	上に
above and below	jōge ni	上下に
behind	ushiro ni	後ろに

line	sen	線
edge of the screen	gamen hashi	画面端
to loop	rūpu suru	ループする

Enemy

enemy	teki	敵
small weak ships	zako teki	ザコ敵
to destroy in one shot	ippatsu de hakai suru	一発で破壊する
high durability	takai taikyūryoku	高い耐久力
enemy ship	tekki	敵機
invincible	muteki	無敵
vulnerable	mubōbi	無防備
vulnerability period	mubōbi na jikan	無防備な時間
enemy bullet	tekidan	敵弾
bullet speed	dansoku	弾速
boss	bosu	ボス
overwhelming	attōteki	圧倒的
weak spot	jakuten	弱点
turret	hōdai	砲台

Enemy Movement

to rotate	kaiten suru	回転する
sine wave	sain kābu	サインカーブ
parabola	hōbutsusen	放物線

multiple directions	fukusū no hōkō	複数の方向
direction	hōkō	方向
three directions	san hōkō	３方向
two directions	ni hōkō	２方向
four directions	yon hōkō	４方向
parallel to	ni sotte	に沿って
to rush (towards)	tosshin suru	突進する
to rush towards your ship	jiki ni mukatte tosshin suru	自機に向かって突進する

Attack and Defense

health	taikyūryoku	耐久力
attack	kōgeki	攻撃
to attack	kōgeki suru	攻撃する
attack power	kōgekiryoku	攻撃力
to receive damage	damēji o ukeru	ダメージを受ける
to shoot	utsu	撃つ
shield	baria	バリア
shield	tate	盾
to disappear	shōshitsu suru	消失する
a set amount of damage	ittei damēji	一定ダメージ
to hit something	ateru	当てる
to be hit by	ataru	当たる
to be hit by enemy bullets	tekidan ni ataru	敵弾に当たる

Life and Respawning

life	ki	機
remaining lives	zanki	残機
restart	sai sutāto	再スタート
to use a life	ki o shōhi suru	機を消費する
to lose a life	misu suru	ミスする
to explode	bakuhatsu suru	爆発する
to respawn	fukkatsu suru	復活する
to respawn where you died	sonoba de fukkatsu suru	その場で復活する
respawn point	fukkatsu chiten	復活地点

Stage and Score

stage	sutēji	ステージ
to complete a stage	sutēji kuria suru	ステージクリアする
score	tokuten	得点
high score	kōtokuten	高得点

Pattern

pattern	patān	パターン
bullet pattern (behavior)	tekidan patān	敵弾パターン
break (in the bullets)	aima	合間
behavior pattern	kōdō patān	行動パターン

to follow	tsuibi suru	追尾する
to avoid	sakeru	避ける

Danmaku

danmaku	danmakukei shūtingu	弾幕系シューティング
gap (in the bullet curtain)	sukima	隙間
a small gap	wazuka na sukima	わずかな隙間
enemy bullet	tekidan	敵弾
to dodge a bullet	tekidan o kaihi suru	敵弾を回避する
to spread (bullet)	furimaku	振りまく
to keep moving	ugoki tsuzukeru	動き続ける
geometric pattern	kikagaku moyō	幾何学模様
pattern (design)	moyō	模様
continuous fire	renzoku shashutsu	連続射出
collision detection	atari hantei	当たり判定

18. Platformer

General

platformer	purattofōmu gēmu	プラットフォームゲーム
2D	nijigen	二次元
sprite	supuraito	スプライト
2.5D	ni ten go jigen	2.5 次元
3D	sanjigen	三次元
scroll	sukurōru	スクロール
side scrolling	yoko sukorōru	横スクロール
auto-scroll	jidō sukurōru	自動スクロール
scroll speed	sukurōru sokudo	スクロール速度

Platforms

platform	ashiba	足場
to get on a platform	ashiba o noru	足場を乗る
to fall off the platform	ashiba kara ochiru	足場から落ちる
edge of the platform	ashiba hashi	足場端
gaps (in between platforms)	sukima	隙間
crumbling platform	kuzureru ashiba	崩れる足場

falling platform	ochiru ashiba	落ちる足場
moving platform	ugoku ashiba	動く足場
sinking platform	shizumu ashiba	沈む足場
floating platform	ukabu ashiba	浮かぶ足場
rotating platform	kaiten suru ashiba	回転する足場
invisible platform	mienai ashiba	見えない足場

Block

block	burokku	ブロック
to hit (e.g. a block)	tataku	叩く
ice block	kōri burokku	氷ブロック
blocks that break if you step on them	noru to kuzureru burokku	乗ると崩れるブロック
unbreakable block	hakai dekinai burokku	破壊できないブロック
breakable block	hakai dekiru burokku	破壊できるブロック

Floor and Ground

floor	yuka	床
ground	jimen	地面
terrain	chikei	地形
slope	saka	坂
stairs	kaidan	階段
falling floor	ochiru yuka	落ちる床

broken floor	kuzureru yuka	崩れる床
disappearing floors	kieru yuka	消える床
moving floors	ugoku jimen	動く地面
icy floor	kōri no yuka	氷の床
slippery floor	numeru yuka	滑る床

Wall

wall	kabe	壁
moving walls	ugoku kabe	動く壁
wall jump	kabe jampu	壁ジャンプ
to wall climb	kabe o noboru	壁を登る

Ceiling

ceiling	tenjō	天井
moving ceiling	ugoku tenjō	動く天井
ceiling that moves up and down	jōge ni ugoku tenjō	上下に動く天井

Other

spring	bane	バネ
ladder	hashigo	はしご

Level

stage / level	sutēji	ステージ
hidden stage	kakushi sutēji	隠しステージ
bonus level	bōnasu sutēji	ボーナスステージ

Hidden

hidden	kakushi	隠し
secret entrance	himitsu no iriguchi	秘密の入り口
hidden area	kakushi eria	隠しエリア
secret area	himitsu no eria	秘密のエリア
hidden stage / level	kakushi sutēji	隠しステージ
secret level	himitsu no sutēji	秘密のステージ

Progression

attempt (at a level)	chōsen	挑戦
time limit	seigenjikan	制限時間
to start over	yarinaosu	やり直す
to restart	sai sutāto suru	再スタートする
to enter (an area)	hairu	入る
stairs	kaidan	階段
path	michi	道
secret path	nukemichi	抜け道

checkpoint	chekku pointo	チェックポイント
beginning a stage	sutēji kaishi	ステージ開始
midway	chūkan	中間
midstage	chūkan sutēji	中間ステージ
second half of the level	kōhan sutēji	後半ステージ
boss stage	bosu sutēji	ボスステージ
boss fight	bosu sen	ボス戦
to complete a stage	sutēji kuria suru	ステージクリアする
time bonus	taimu bōnasu	タイムボーナス
next level	tsuginaru sutēji	次なるステージ

Stage Elements

stage element	shikake	仕掛け
trap	torappu	トラップ
obstacle	shōgaibutsu	障害物
an obstacle is in the way	shōgaibutsu ga jama	障害物が邪魔
to avoid an obstacle	shōgaibutsu o sakeru	障害物を避ける
spikes	toge	トゲ
terrain	chikei	地形
wall	kabe	壁
to block the path	michi o fusagu	道をふさぐ
moving walls	ugoku kabe	動く壁
moving floors	ugoku jimen	動く地面
moving ceiling	ugoku tenjō	動く天井

ceiling that moves up and down	jōge ni ugoku tenjō	上下に動く天井
to get caught between	hasamareru	挟まれる
to be crushed to death	asshi suru	圧死する
disappearing floors	kieru yuka	消える床

Lives

life	ki	機
remaining lives	zanki	残機
to use a life	ki o shōhi suru	機を消費する
to lose a life	misu suru	ミスする
instantly lose a life	soku misu	即ミス

Ways to Lose a Life

to die instantly (e.g. going out of bounds)	sokushi suru	即死する
to fall	rakka suru	落下する
fall damage	rakka damēji	落下ダメージ
to fall to your death	rakkashi suru	落下死する
to fall in the water	mizu ni ochiru	水に落ちる
to be crushed to death	asshi suru	圧死する

to be blown up (and lose a life)	bakushi suru	爆死する

Enemy

enemy	teki	敵
to avoid an enemy	teki o sakeru	敵を避ける
to touch an enemy	teki ni fureru	敵に触れる

Item

key	kagi	カギ
treasure	zaihō	財宝
collectible	shūshū aitemu	収集アイテム
powerup	pawā appu	パワーアップ
invincible	muteki	無敵
falling item	rakka chū aitemu	落下中アイテム
floating item	fuyū aitemu	浮遊アイテム
to appear on the stage	sutēji ni shutsugen suru	ステージに出現する

Movement

to move	idō suru	移動する
to move right	migi ni ugoku	右に動く

to move left	hidari ni ugoku	左に動く
to move left and right	sayū ni ugoku	左右に動く
to scroll forward	sukurōru o susumeru	スクロールを進める
to crouch	shagamu	しゃがむ
to walk	aruku	歩く
to run	hashiru	走る
to swim	oyogu	泳ぐ
to slide	suberu	滑る
to slide into	suberikomu	滑り込む
to step on something	fumu	踏む
jump	jampu	ジャンプ
high jump	takai jampu	高いジャンプ
double jump	nidan jampu	２段ジャンプ
to float	fuyū suru	浮遊する
to fall	rakka suru	落下する
fall damage	rakka damēji	落下ダメージ
fall speed	rakka sokudo	落下速度
climb	noboru	登る
to wall climb	kabe o noboru	壁を登る
wall jump	kabe jampu	壁ジャンプ
to glide	kakkū suru	滑空する
to grab onto	tsukamaru	捕まる
vines	tsuru	つる
rope	rōpu	ロープ
to climb a rope	rōpu o noboru	ロープを登る
to get off	oriru	降りる

to push	osu	押す
to pull	hiku	引く

Misc

edge of the screen	gamenhashi	画面端
tile	masu	マス
one-tile-wide gap	ichi masu no sukima	1マスの隙間
timer	taimā	タイマー
to break the timer	taimā o kowasu	タイマーを壊す

19. Small Sections

Falling Block

puzzle game	pazuru gēmu	パズルゲーム
falling block game	ochimono gēmu	落ち物ゲーム
falling block game	ochi gē	落ちゲー
field	fīrudo	フィールド
top row	sai jōdan	最上段
block	burokku	ブロック
to drop	doroppu suru	ドロップする
fall speed	rakka sokudo	落下速度
to pile up	tsumu	積む
to rotate	kaiten suru	回転する
chain	rensa	連鎖
to disappear	kieru	消える
to clear	kesu	消す
to match	sorou	揃う
horizontal	yoko	横
vertical	tate	縦
diagonal	naname	斜め
cleared blocks	keshita burokku	消したブロック
same color	onaji iro	同じ色
same color	dōshoku	同色
opponent	aite	相手
to hinder	bōgai suru	妨害する

Freemium Terms

mobile game	mobairu gēmu	モバイルゲーム
smartphone game	sumaho gē	スマホゲー
app	apuri	アプリ
free	muryō	無料
free game	muryō gēmu	無料ゲーム
free download	muryō daunrōdo	無料ダウンロード
game that costs money	yūryō gēmu	有料ゲーム
freemium	furīmiamu	フリーミアム
free to play	kihon purei muryō	基本プレイ無料
free to play	kihon muryō	基本無料
trial version	taikenban	体験版
full version	kanzenban	完全版
free version	muryōban	無料版
restrictions	seigen	制限
premium	puremiamu	プレミアム
paid for item	kakin yōso	課金要素
loot box	rūto bokkusu	ルートボックス
rare item	rea aitemu	レアアイテム
special item	tokubetsu aitemu	特別アイテム
microtransaction	aitemu kakin	アイテム課金
monthly fee	getsugaku kakin	月額課金
subscription	sabusukuripushon	サブスクリプション
in-game advertising	gēmunai kōkoku	ゲーム内広告
in-game item	gēmu nai aitemu	ゲーム内アイテム
in-game purchase	gēmu nai kōnyū	ゲーム内購入

in-game currency	gēmu nai tsūka	ゲーム内通貨
stamina	sutamina	スタミナ
cosmetic (armor)	sōshoku	装飾
login bonus	roguin bōnasu	ログインボーナス
additional content	tsuika kontentsu	追加コンテンツ

CPSIA information can be obtained
at www.ICGtesting.com
Printed in the USA
LVHW050148250621
691124LV00001B/202